LORD, TEACH ME WISDOM

To Dee Moen, now with God

And to all the wise
      dedicated
      Navigator women
   whom God has led to single life . . .

Women who do not build
      through husband
      or children
But by a sacrificial
      outpouring
      of themselves;

Women whose lives
      are truly
   a monument to building.

Carole Mayhall is the author of *From the Heart of a Woman* (NavPress, 1976) and—with her husband, Jack—*Marriage Takes More than Love* (NavPress, 1978).

After growing up in a small town in southern Michigan, she graduated from Wheaton College in Wheaton, Illinois, with a degree in Christian education. She served as education director for a church in Ohio before marrying Jack.

The Mayhalls later joined the staff of The Navigators, and Jack now serves as the United States director. They have lived and ministered in various communities throughout the United States, and have spoken at seminars and conferences around the world.

The Mayhalls live in Colorado Springs. Their daughter, Lynn, is married to Navigator staff member Tim Westberg.

Contents

A Search Begun with Prayer

THE PHONE RANG IMPERATIVELY, and I dashed in from the yard, a trowel in my mud-caked hand. My sister's voice was trembly-sounding and far away.

"I just got home from the doctor," she said. "You know I've been having pains in my head and chest for a few weeks, but the doctor couldn't find anything wrong. Today I noticed a lump on my neck, and when I went in to be checked, the doctor took another X ray and sent me to a specialist. After his examination, he told me I should enter the hospital immediately. He thinks it is serious."

I sank to the floor, clutching the phone, fighting the sinking feeling inside me. "What do you mean, *serious*?"

"He wouldn't come right out and say. Just that he would advise immediate hospitalization and it was 'very serious.' I said I couldn't go in right away. I've just got too many things to finish. We're redecorating the apartment upstairs, my back room is a mess, and . . . ."

"Oh, Joye!" My voice was choked with tears. "Those things aren't important. Please do what the doctor advises and let's find out what it is."

11

As I hung up the phone that June afternoon in 1977, panic poked a gaping hole in my peace. "Lord, not my sister! Just two months ago You took Mom. And Joye is such a vivacious, loving wife and mother—so vital. She is growing spiritually and serving You with all her heart. I love her so. Not Joye, Lord, *please*."

The next four days were a nightmare of tests and more tests. We anxiously kept in touch twice a day by phone. I didn't want to be home in Colorado when she was in an Indiana hospital, but there was nothing to be done until the tests were concluded. For me, those days were filled with tears. Jack, my husband, spent much time just comforting me. I made reservations to fly out to be with Joye the day after her biopsy.

Then the diagnosis was confirmed—cancer. Joye had acute lymphatic leukemia, a rare disease among adults. Yet my father died, at age 57, only six days after receiving an identical diagnosis. The reality of Joye's illness destroyed my last vestiges of self-control and unleashed a torrent of crippling fear and pain.

I was a basket case! I couldn't speak without crying. I couldn't think about Christmas, blueberry jam, home-canned pickles, or antiques, all of which were intimately connected in my mind with my sister. And I was flying to her the next day to *help*. How could I help in the condition I was in?

The night was warmly soft as I slipped out onto our small upstairs porch. I needed help desperately.

"Lord, help me," I pleaded. "I need You more now than I've ever needed You. I need Your strength, Your grace, Your comfort. You *promised* to be my strength when I am weak, and I am claiming that promise right now." My flood of words suddenly evaporated along with my tears, and I went inside to bed—and to sleep.

The next morning I flew to Indiana, but what a difference! Instead of turbulence, there was peace. Instead of my shakiness, God's strength. Instead of anxiety, comfort and grace.

Joye was death-gray and perspiring when I entered her hospital room. Blue-black circles framed eyes closed in weariness and pain. A swathe of white bandage encased her neck where the biopsy was performed. The day before, I would have started weeping again, but now I felt a comforting strength that obviously was not mine.

During the week that followed, even while holding Joye's hands during an excruciatingly painful spinal tap, my heart was supernaturally, unexplicably *calm*.

For Joye and for all of us who were with her every waking moment—her husband Fred, Melody her daughter, and myself—there was abundant, abounding grace. Not just a little grace; not just enough to "squeak through" those agonizing days—but a full, triumphant, glorious grace: a grace spelled *j-o-y*. A pervading peace made it a week of glory. God's strength lifted our hearts in praise. It was a week of miracles in all our hearts.

Every year back at Wheaton College, our president, Dr. V. Raymond Edman, would give a chapel message on the theme, "Not Somehow, but Triumphantly." I thought of this many times during that week, for God was measuring out His grace, not just somehow, but in a truly *triumphant* way.

One evening Jan, a senior student nurse, came into Joye's room and asked nervously if she could interview Joye on how she felt about her diagnosis. Jan was in a two-week "stress course." It was her job to interview terminally ill patients to see if she could help them by "listening out" their fears and anger.

An inner radiance illuminated Joye's pale face as she

talked. "Jan, I'm not afraid of death. Oh, I'm somewhat fearful of the process and pain of dying, but I know that death only means a change of residence for me. As a result of receiving Jesus Christ into my life, and experiencing His forgiveness for my sins, I have full assurance that when I die, I will go to heaven and be with God for all eternity."

For the next 45 minutes Joye told Jan about Christ and made the "way of the Cross" plain to Jan. When Jan left she said, "I came in here to see if I could help you, but you have helped me. I've learned some things to share with others who aren't handling their illness as well as you are. Thank you."

As I listened to Joye share her faith with Jan, the words of Psalm 90:12 nudged me sharply: "Teach us to number our days that we may present to Thee a heart of wisdom."

"Lord, You have given Joye a 'heart of wisdom.' I see it . . . I feel it . . . I know it. Thank You. She is wise and will present to You that heart full of wisdom when she meets You face to face.

"Lord, that is what I desire with all my heart. Teach *me* . . . teach me to number my days, be they few or many, and help me present to You at the end of my life a *heart of wisdom*."

Thoughts converged, collided, dissected and then came together in a jumble in my mind. What were the implications of my prayer? What really *is* wisdom, and how do I obtain it? Will I have it only at the end of my life, or do I learn some of it each day in a continuing process? Can such wisdom be taught to others, or do we all have to learn for ourselves and be individually taught by God? If God builds wisdom into my life, what is my responsibility to those around me? Though I had made a sporadic study of wisdom, I had no answers to these new questions. But I determined to look for them.

PART ONE
Wisdom's Ways

1 Wisdom and Knowledge

"HELP, LORD. What do we do now?" I prayed. In two days Joye's doctor was going to begin a course of treatment which, once started, would be irreversible. Was it the right one?

Her doctor, a specialist in leukemia, told us honestly that he had treated only one other adult patient who had the same rare form of the disease Joye had. We consulted another specialist who advocated a radically different form of treatment.

The time for making a decision was short. We received conflicting advice—both to leave her in the hands of the nearby doctor, and to fly her to a cancer clinic elsewhere immediately. We were all so caught up in our own emotions, it was impossible to be objective or calm.

Doing something—*anything*—seemed imperative, since we felt so helpless. I telephoned four Christian doctor friends and asked them this question: "I need some advice from you first as a Christian, then as a husband, and lastly as a doctor. If your wife had acute lymphatic leukemia, what would you choose as the course of treatment?"

Since my father died of leukemia 20 years ago, vast research has been done and much knowledge gained. But a great deal still needs to be learned. I found that there are almost as many variations of treatment as there are hospitals treating the disease. One well-known clinic tries to kill the disease by massive doses of new experimental medicines given mainly in one week's time. Another spreads part of the same treatment over an extended period. One theory says that leukemia cells "hide" in the brain during a remission period, and suggests radiation to the brain to kill the cancer cells; another says this treatment is no longer considered feasible for adults. The variety of advice was confusing.

My doctor friends expressed concern and support. Three of the four said they personally would keep their wives at home for treatment nearby. The ultimate decision, of course, rested with Fred and Joye.

At that moment we were frustrated with the lack of knowledge in the medical field concerning this disease. Without precise knowledge, deciding what to do was beyond human capability.

A prerequisite of wisdom is knowledge. One has to know about something (knowledge) before one can take a proper course of action (wisdom). Knowledge is defined as "knowing something with familiarity gained through experience or association" and "the fact or condition of being aware of something."[1] And wisdom is defined as the "ability to discern inner qualities and relationships, insight; good sense, judgment."[2]

I reflected that King Solomon asked God for both wisdom and knowledge (see 2 Chronicles 1:10), and God responded that his choice was a good one. In fact, God said it was such a good choice that He would give Solomon not only wisdom and knowledge, but also the riches and honor he hadn't asked for! (2 Chronicles 1:12).

In this beautiful account we find that wisdom and knowledge are integrally associated with understanding and discernment. The same story recorded in 1 Kings 3 tells us that Solomon asked for "an understanding heart" to judge the people (verse 9). God rephrased Solomon's request in His reply. He said that because Solomon asked for "discernment [or 'hearing'] to understand justice, behold I have given you a wise and discerning heart" (verses 11-12).

If ever we needed discernment, we needed it to decide which course of treatment was best for Joye. And while man's knowledge of this rare form of cancer is extremely limited, God's wisdom and knowledge is total! He led Fred and Joye to choose treatment by the doctor close to them, the doctor who had treated only one other adult with the disease. But they prayed, with many others, that this doctor would be given wisdom to use the method of treatment which would be *best for her*. We saw God do miracles in guiding that doctor. Let me tell you about just one.

Joye was not only weak and ill but also extremely sensitive to pain from so many injections and blood tests, and her biopsy. But in order to find out if her disease was in remission, another bone marrow test had to be done, along with the first injection into the spine of a chemotherapy drug—both tremendously painful procedures that had to be done without an anesthetic. We began to pray the week before that God would deliver her from fear and give her strength. He did much more than that!

That Tuesday morning, two nurses stood by the doctor to hold Joye still during the bone marrow test. But they were not needed. As the doctor drilled through the chest bone, Joye was supposed to feel a "drawing sensation" when the needle penetrated the marrow. But God was so sustaining her, so protecting her, that not only was she feeling *no pain at all*, she couldn't even feel the needle in the marrow. The doctor had to wiggle it around a bit in order to be sure he had placed it correctly!

As he proceeded to the spinal injection, which was to be the first of four weekly injections, God again blocked the pain.

We were thankful and thrilled to see what God could do. The next week we prayed that God again would block the pain of the injection. He didn't. Instead, it took the doctor three attempts before the spinal needle would penetrate. Joye had a very difficult time of it.

"Why, Lord?" I asked. "I know You give only good gifts to Your children. We knew last week was a good gift, but can this be good?"

As we learned, God doesn't always show us the "whys" of our trials. Some questions will be answered only on the Other Side when we learn more about His purposes. But this time, God enabled us to see at least a glimmer of what He had done. That day, Joye's doctor decided to cancel the two remaining injections. We couldn't help thinking it was because of the difficulty of the second injection.

We knew then, and can certainly see in retrospect, that this was God's way of giving Joye's doctor wisdom as to how to treat her. She went into a strong, year-long remission, so in her case the four doses might have been too much.

Many times in my life I have clung to the promise in James 1:5: "But if any of you lacks wisdom, let him ask of God, who gives to all men generously and without reproach, and it will be given to him." I am so grateful for the way God answers my requests. My wisdom is minimal at best. I need His wisdom daily, and hourly.

God does tell us, however, to increase our *knowledge*

so we will gain in wisdom. "A wise man will hear and increase in learning," Solomon said (Proverbs 1:5). Knowledge is to be sought diligently!

"My son, if you will receive my sayings,
And treasure my commandments within you,
Make your ear attentive to wisdom,
Incline your heart to understanding;
For if you cry for discernment,
Lift your voice for understanding;
If you seek her as silver,
And search for her as for hidden treasures;
Then you will discern the fear of the Lord,
And discover the knowledge of God.
For the Lord gives wisdom;
From His mouth come knowledge and understanding."
—(Proverbs 2:1-6)

Notice the active verbs in this passage: receive, treasure, incline, cry, seek, search. We are to pursue wisdom and search for knowledge. And yet the knowledge and wisdom, and even the search for them, are all wrapped up in *God Himself*. We are to search for wisdom, but the Lord gives it (verse 6). We are to cry for it, but the fear of the Lord is wisdom and knowledge (Proverbs 1:7).

One can have knowledge without wisdom. But knowledge alone is not enough. In fact, knowledge by itself can be harmful. Paul said that "knowledge makes arrogant" (1 Corinthians 8:1). However, this passage from Proverbs states that one of the requirements for gaining wisdom is the knowledge upon which to act. So I must seek knowledge not for intellect's sake, but for wisdom.

That insight was helpful. In the case of my sister, we gathered all the knowledge we could accumulate in those brief days before a decision had to be made, and then prayed for wisdom in order to act on that limited knowledge and make the correct choice.

My search for God's wisdom, then, becomes partly a seeking of more *knowledge* of Him—who He is, and the where, what, and how of His working—both in the past and in my life now. This points a finger directly to my time spent with God in His Word, searching for Him as for hidden treasure, seeing Him with my whole heart.

Father, God,
I need Your help in this.
Please give me a heart to know You . . .
   the discipline to seek You . . .
      a hunger for Your every Word.
Thank You.

---

1. By permission. From *Webster's New Collegiate Dictionary* © 1979 by G. and C. Merriam Co., publishers of the Merriam-Webster Dictionaries, page 639.
2. *Webster's New Collegiate Dictionary*, page 1345.

2 Wisdom + Knowledge = Understanding

I FELT THE EDGES of my strength begin to crumble. Peace started to fade into the horizon of pain. I realized then that God had given me a 100-pound sack of His grace to get through the first weeks of Joye's illness, "not somehow, but triumphantly." But today I awakened fearful and weak again, on the verge of tears. I had used up the last of the 100-pound sackful. What should I do? How could I keep going?

And then I remembered: "*Daily* will I help thee."

God's grace had not been used up. It is fathomless—inexhaustible. In those weeks I had not had the time or energy to continually call upon Him for His grace. God knew that, and so He gave me an abundant supply. But now God wanted the closeness of my moment-by-moment *dependence*—asking so He could freely give and give and give again. I would remain weak if I refused to depend on Him and ask Him for the grace to be at peace, to be joyful, and to be calm.

I prayed then, *"Oh Lord,*
Thank You for Your 100-pound sacks of grace.

But thank You, too, for the daily measure,
  always sufficient.

                    Amen."

It was a new glimmer of understanding in my life, a fresh lesson from the hand of the Master Teacher, and I was grateful. *Understanding* is a course He knows I need! And many of the incidents God uses to teach us understanding are unforgettable.

On one such occasion we were enjoying a few days of rest and study at our friends' beautiful summer home. Not being accustomed to the new electric ranges (mine takes ages to warm up), I set some oil for popcorn on a burner and went into the living room to tell Jack something. It was *only* a moment, but upon returning to the kitchen I discovered the oil had burst into flames and the copper hood over the stove was on fire! I screamed for Jack and reached for the pan and a towel at the same time. Putting the pan down hastily in the sink, I frantically beat at the flaming hood as Jack reached the kitchen to help. In a moment the fire was out—but the damage had been done. The beautiful copper hood was no longer beautiful. It was black. Soot had turned the ceiling gray and greasy.

The next morning we tried to wash the ceiling and walls but only succeeded in leaving a line of demarcation where we had washed—and the soot wasn't coming off completely anyway. I was depressed as I phoned my friend Lois to tell her what had happened, more unhappy than if it had been my own kitchen.

Lois's lilting voice was reassuring and sympathetic and I had to stop right there and thank God for Christian friends. It was as if Lois and her husband had been able to put themselves in our place and truly understand.

However, in the next two days of our stay every time I saw or thought of that blackened copper hood, I despaired. We had been trusted with another's property and had damaged it.

Later I read with great empathy about a young seminary student in another country who was chopping wood to build a dormitory. In his energetic pursuit, the head of his borrowed axe flew from its handle and landed in the middle of the river. He was terrified, for he had no money to buy an axe to replace it. He rushed to his professor nearby and told him what had happened.

The professor wasn't at all shaken. "Where did you lose it?" he asked, and the young student pointed to the spot where the axe head had fallen. The professor then did a strange thing. He cut a stick from a tree and threw it into the water. I wonder if the student thought, "What good will *that* do?"

Imagine the student's astonishment when the axe head rose from the river and attached itself to the stick!

"Grab it!" the teacher said. You may be sure the student did exactly that! (see 2 Kings 6:1-7).

As I read this story of how God used Elisha (the professor) to perform a miracle for a borrowed *axe head*, I was filled with wonder. Our God is big enough to be concerned about the "littles" in our lives. In the midst of raising people from the dead, curing lepers, and winning wars (see 2 Kings 4-6), God saw fit to show us that He understands our concern for things like a borrowed axe head!

Throughout the Bible we see that the God of wisdom is completely understanding. He sympathizes with our weaknesses (Hebrews 4:15) and is merciful and faithful (Hebrews 2:17-18). He can put Himself in our place to understand us *because He was one of us.*

I look at my God who totally understands—and I worship.

But then I look at myself. And when I look at myself, I get discouraged. So many times I am not understanding—of people, of situations, of spiritual truths. So the question comes to me time and time again, *how* can I become an understanding person—understanding like my friend Lois, but even more than that, understanding like God?

Before I can answer, I have to know what understanding is.

To understand means "to grasp the meaning of," "to grasp the reasonableness of," or "to show a sympathetic or tolerant attitude toward something."[1] My own definition is simply, "the ability to put yourself in the place of another."

The sun came out from under a large bank of clouds and I automatically reached around under my legs for my sunglasses in my purse beneath the car seat.

Suddenly all my nerves came to attention as I frantically searched for my purse. Nothing! We were on our way back home after a week's vacation, and I said desperately, "Jack! I can't find my purse!"

He pulled quickly to the side of the road and we began our hunt through the car. I thought, *"Horrors! Not much cash but many credit cards, keys, driver's license . . . ."*

"I must have left it at McDonald's when we stopped there for lunch," I surmised. "What a silly thing to do!" I chided myself.

Instead of saying, "Yes, it *was* a stupid thing to do. How come you can't remember your purse? Why did you take it in anyway?" he said, "I'm so sorry. I do know how you feel."

We pulled off the interstate into the first filling station. Some husbands would have slouched in the car and said, "Well, hurry up and call. We haven't got all day."

Jack quietly took charge. *He* called McDonald's and cushioned the news that nothing had been turned in there.

As we drove the rest of the way home, we prayed about it together. We had seen God help us find contact lenses lost in sawdust by our daughter Lynn, and we had seen Him take care of our possessions and guard our safety; we knew He could care for one brown purse.

Some husbands would have given their wives instructions: "When we get home you'll have to call the credit card companies. Tomorrow you can call the locksmith." Jack said, "I love you. We'll take care of it."

When we returned home, he called a tennis resort where we had stopped. Then he checked back with McDonald's once more before beginning the credit card calling. To our great relief, the purse had been found intact and was in their safe. We thanked God for once again protecting us.

That evening as I reflected on the incident, two things were prominent: an overwhelming love for a husband who was so kind, and a realization of Jack's *understanding*. Jack had put himself in my shoes and truly understood. Because of this, he acted in a loving and considerate way.

The ability to put yourself in the place of another—to comprehend how they are feeling—is a great part of understanding. Lois and Dean had been able to do this when we blackened their lovely kitchen. Jack had done this when I lost my purse. God does this every moment of our lives.

The origin of the word *understand* is interesting:

"Five hundred years ago one could have talked about 'understanding (standing under) a tree in a rainstorm.' As one of Shakespeare's characters put it, 'Why, stand under and understand is all one.' Today, however, only the figurative meaning is used, and to *understand* means to have a comprehension or awareness of something or its meaning (as if one knew something from the bottom up, from having *stood under* it).''[2]

I like that! Understanding is to "see things from the bottom up . . . to stand under"—to really put yourself in the place of another, and to comprehend. Understanding is not just close kin to wisdom, but an integral part of it. Solomon said, "Wisdom is in the presence of the one who has understanding" (Proverbs 17:24).

On the one hand it is apparent that the Lord is the one to give us understanding and wisdom. "For the Lord gives wisdom; from His mouth come knowledge and understanding" (Proverbs 2:6). On the other hand, I am to seek His knowledge so that I may have understanding, for "the knowledge of the Holy One is understanding" (Proverbs 9:10).

The truth seen from God's side shows that He gives wisdom when we pray for it, and when we know Christ, who *is* wisdom. Paul prayed for the Christians at Ephesus "that the God of our Lord Jesus Christ, the Father of glory, may give unto you the spirit of wisdom and revelation *in the knowledge of him*, the eyes of your understanding being enlightened" (Ephesians 1:17-18, KJV). We know that Christ is our wisdom, for Paul wrote, "By His doing you are in Christ Jesus, who became to us wisdom from God, and righteousness and sanctification, and redemption" (1 Corinthians 1:30).

The truth from man's side reveals that we must *search* for wisdom as for hidden treasures (see Proverbs 2:1-5).

While studying Proverbs, I discovered I couldn't separate knowledge, wisdom, and understanding into component parts. Every time I thought I had it figured out, a verse would erase the distinctiveness. "The fear of the Lord is the beginning of *knowledge*" we read in Proverbs 1:7. But in Proverbs 9:10 we learn, "The fear of the Lord is the beginning of *wisdom*, and the *knowledge* of the Holy One is *understanding.*" And in Proverbs 15:33, "The fear of the Lord is the instruction for wisdom." These characteristics are unique, but like flour, water, and yeast put together to form bread, once baked they cannot be separated. But my mind needed to examine the separate ingredients before digesting the whole loaf. After meditating on these truths I concluded that knowledge of God—heart knowledge which comes through searching the Word and praying—results in God *giving* wisdom, and with knowledge and wisdom come understanding. If I seek knowledge of God in His Word and in my everyday happenings, if I search for His wisdom like hidden treasures, understanding should be a natural, growing thing in my life—a by-product of the other two. Understanding is all wrapped up in letting the God of understanding fill my life with Himself. As my roots "go down deep into the soil of God's marvelous love" (Ephesians 3:17, LB), as I see the full extent of the love of Christ, *then* I shall be filled up with God Himself. My part is to search for His treasures and stay open to His filling. His part is to give me His understanding and wisdom.

---

1. *Webster's New Collegiate Dictionary*, pages 1275-1276.
2. *Reader's Digest Family Word Finder* (Pleasantville, New York: Readers' Digest Association, Inc., 1975), page 834. Used by permission.

3 Knowing the God of Wisdom

SHE STOOD WITH HER HUSBAND and tall son in the middle of a Brazilian shopping center. Crowds were pressing around them, but to her, the three were on an island of aloneness. Their attempts to communicate were breaking against the reefs of the language barrier.

A silent, desperate prayer tore from her heart. "Lord, what are we to do? The plane leaves in a few hours for the jungles of the Amazon. Even the people who speak *some* English cannot understand that we need contact solution for Bobby's eyes. You know that with his eye disease, he *has* to have that solution. But no one understands us. Help us, please."

Americans alone. She had stopped several Brazilians, but even those who knew some English were unable to translate "contact solution," and the druggists too were unable to comprehend her need.

As she prayed, a well-dressed Brazilian came toward her and she made one more faltering attempt. "Sir, do you speak English?" she asked.

He stopped abruptly and smiled. "Yes, I do. May I help you?"

The next half hour was incredible. He was a minister in the Brazilian government with an important cabinet meeting in 30 minutes. But not only could he understand the family's need, he offered to drive them to a doctor who was a contact lens specialist. When a hurried trip across town found the office closed he took them to the only place in Brasilia where the particular solution could be obtained—the pharmacy of the Medical Center. There the Brazilian minister phoned the doctor at his home to check the type of solution, purchased it, and then refused to be repaid by the Americans! Insisting he still had time to make his meeting, he drove them back to the shopping center to catch a bus to the airport. When they effusively thanked him, he replied, "I have been waiting several years for this opportunity. When I was in the United States a few years ago someone was especially kind to me, and I have been looking for an opportunity to return that kindness to an American ever since."

God's timing is incredible!

One December, Jack and I were praying about whether I should accompany him on a business trip to Germany the following April. At long last it seemed there were no obstacles. Our daughter was married and we had saved enough so that I could go on the trip—something we had been looking forward to for some time. But as we prayed about it, we received a very definite "no" from God. Truthfully, I was upset to think God would say no when we had planned this for so long. I couldn't quite understand it because I know God delights to delight us. But it *was* a very definite "no!"

After Jack's plans were finalized, I was asked to speak to a women's conference in Michigan during the time he would be away so I made plans to visit my sister and mother just prior to the conference.

As I walked in from church on a Sunday, the day before I was to fly to Michigan, the phone was ringing. It was my sister. "Mother has had a massive stroke," she said. "The doctor says you should come as soon as possible."

I already had my ticket. It was just a matter of changing the flight. I already had a person to come and stay in our home. She just had to come one night early. I already had a clear schedule. God had seen to that.

But He didn't stop there. Lynn and Tim, our daughter and her husband who lived in Champaign, Illinois, just "happened" to be in Chicago that weekend. They were able to meet my plane, drive me to Michigan, and be the wonderful support that Jack couldn't be during this difficult time.

Arriving at my sister's hometown we immediately went to the hospital (it was the middle of the night but the kind nurses let us in). Mother roused slightly but was under heavy sedation. We stayed with her for a few minutes before going to my sister's home and planned to return to the hospital early the next morning.

Mother lived for eight hours that Monday and I was privileged to be with her during that time. Just after Joye arrived in the afternoon, Mother stirred. It was as if she was waiting to say goodbye to Joye, who had cared for her for so long. Because of the stroke, her facial muscles were paralyzed on one side and she had not been able to smile. But as she roused, she *smiled*. Her expressive brown eyes opened wide. Then she went into the presence of her King.

Joye, Lynn, Tim, and I joined hands and prayed. We thanked God for a wonderful Mother who demonstrated Christ to us. We rejoiced through our tears that she was home with Jesus—and with her husband whom she loved so dearly.

And I too was able to say goodbye. I wouldn't have missed that for the world—certainly not for a trip to Europe! God had said no so He could be gracious to me. His timing couldn't have been more perfect. Jack, because of plane schedules, was able to make it back for only the last part of the time at the funeral parlor and for the funeral itself. If I had been with him . . . .

Our times are in God's hands. I see this all around me—in my life, in friends' lives, and in God's Word.

At first I couldn't understand why the Holy Spirit chose to include in Scripture the story of the Shunammite woman's house and land. It appears to be such a simple story. Or is it?

Elisha had healed the son of a Shunammite woman (we don't even know her name!) and had befriended her through the years (see 2 Kings 4:8-37). One day he persuaded her to take her family and leave the country because there would be a famine for seven years (2 Kings 8:1). Upon her return after the seven-year period, someone else had taken possession of her home and land. The "finders-keepers" rule must have applied back then. So she went to the king to appeal for her property (2 Kings 8:3-6).

Now can you imagine the influence a Shunammite woman would have had with a king? Probably none at all.

But in God's timing, at the exact moment she entered the palace, Elisha's servant was waxing eloquent to the king concerning his master's miracles—including the one in which he had raised from death the Shunammite woman's son. Looking up, the servant exclaimed, "Oh, here she comes now!" The king asked her to tell him about it herself. Obviously impressed, he restored not only her home and land, but also the proceeds from her crops during the seven years she had been out of the country! I really don't think her visit could have been timed any better!

'God is not limited by time. He sees the end from the beginning. A day to Him is as a thousand years. Yet even in our human time frame He acts with accuracy.

As we search for knowledge of God, we do it primarily in two ways. First and foremost, we seek Him in His Word. When I read of His amazing timing in the details of a Shunammite woman, I marvel at God's love, His interest, and His astonishing precision.

Second, we see the knowledge and wisdom of God as He operates in our lives and in the lives of those around us. As I heard of my friends' experience in Brazil, I could not fail to worship the God who *cares that much!*

Jeremiah wrote, "Thus says the Lord, 'Let not a wise man boast of his wisdom, and let not the mighty man boast of his might, let not a rich man boast of his riches; but let him who boasts boast of this, that he understands and knows Me, that I am the Lord who exercises lovingkindness, justice, and righteousness on earth; for I delight in these things,' declares the Lord" (Jeremiah 9:23-24).

To *know* God. The haze was fast dissolving as I began to see that the beginning of wisdom really is the fear of the Lord, and that knowing Him is understanding.

4 Obtaining Wisdom

A KING-SIZE BED is far too big when one is in it all by oneself!

I tossed and turned, trying for sleep. Jack was overseas and I was lonely. The house was too quiet. Even the wind was still. I tried praying, quoting Scripture, and thinking of clouds drifting. But sleep eluded me.

The forlorn emptiness of the bed's white expanse forced me to sit up and turn on the light. I had just been reading a book* that suggested reading five Psalms each night starting with the one numbered the same as the day of the month, and choosing the other four by adding 30, 60, 90, and 120 to the date. There are 150 Psalms, so a 30-day month completes the book. The author suggests this would be a good thing to do before going to sleep, so one could meditate on the Psalms subconsciously while sleeping. I took that to mean it might put me to sleep! So I thought I would try it.

Meditation: The Bible Tells You How by Jim Downing (Colorado Springs: NavPress, 1976).

To say it failed to help me sleep would be an understatement. In fact, I got so excited about the wondrous things God showed me, I had a hard time sleeping all night! But it was certainly worth every minute of wakefulness.

It was the sixth day of October, so I read the sixth Psalm without finding anything special for my situation. When I read the 36th Psalm next, however, I sat straight up in bed. I read, "They drink their fill of the abundance of Thy house; and Thou dost give them to drink of the river of Thy delights" (36:8).

And God put this picture into my mind:

He was sitting on His throne, and from His throne was flowing a great, wide, deep, sparkling river—the river of His delights. He was smiling and inviting me to drink.

I was standing on the bank of this wonderful river of delights, getting very thirsty. So I finally reached into my pocket and got out a little demitasse spoon, dipped it into the river, and took a sip. After a while I became thirsty again, so once more I took a spoonful from the river.

God smiled as He spoke, "Carole, why don't you really *drink*?" He asked. "Look down beside you. There is a great big ten-gallon container. Pick it up and drink fully—or better yet, why don't you just jump right in My river and let it flow all over you?"

I want to drink deeply, fully, and freely of His river of delights. He wants me to drink. But often I am satisfied with so little—a demitasse spoonful.

"Lord," I prayed, "give me an insatiable thirst for Your delights, a hunger for Your righteousness, and a continual desire to have more of You Yourself."

God is the Source. He is the source of delight and the source of wisdom. Only as we have Him will we be wise and fulfilled.

What I had suspected all along was confirmed now in my mind. Wisdom starts with God and continues as we experience God in Christ. I read, "But by His doing you are in Christ Jesus, who became to us wisdom from God, and righteousness and sanctification, and redemption" (1 Corinthians 1:30).

My longing to be a wise and understanding person, therefore, begins and ends with God Himself. I accept that, but how do I take it from "up there" into the "down here" in my life?

As I continued reading Psalm 36, I read, "For with Thee is the fountain of life; in Thy light we see light" (36:9).

It came to me then! It is only by the Holy Spirit's illuminating power that we comprehend the light or truths from the Word of God. I have a two-fold responsibility: to open the Book, and to avail myself completely of the Holy Spirit's guidance. If I am closed to the Holy Spirit's teaching, even though my Bible is open, I won't understand it.

Scripture tells us not to quench or grieve the Spirit. But God has promised to give us the mighty inner strengthening of His Holy Spirit. As we confess our sins and walk in obedience to His voice, we will be opening ourselves to the light of the Spirit. The Holy Spirit will tell us to open the Word. As we do this, as we search the Word diligently, He will illuminate our minds and hearts and teach us to drink deeply of God's delights.

I have the ability to "turn off" that light by blocking the Spirit and by keeping the Book closed. God will not force His wisdom on me, or force me to use what He has already given. I must open my mind to Him by memorizing and meditating on Scripture, I must open my heart to Him by praying, and I must open my life to Him by spending time in His Word and letting His Word dwell in me. If I keep that light turned on, His wisdom will begin to operate in my life.

It is frightening to me to realize that the wisest king of all, Solomon, at one point in his life became a foolish man. God gave wisdom to Solomon, a wisdom that was accepted and used, resulting in prosperity, riches, and peace. Still, *Solomon turned off the light!* He disobeyed God by marrying heathen women who led him to build temples to their gods. Eventually this led Solomon completely away from God. "Solomon was no longer interested in the Lord God of Israel who had appeared to him twice to warn him specifically against worshiping other gods. But he hadn't listened" (1 Kings 11:10, LB).

Wisdom, I was seeing, comes from being open to the teaching of the Holy Spirit, from opening our lives to His Word, and from obeying His voice. These truths were being clarified in my mind. But I knew it was only a beginning.

5 Hearing—A Requirement for Wisdom

MY THOUGHTS TODAY are just as thick and hazy as the fog outside my window. I have been grappling with a truth that's complex. I feel as if I'm stumbling around in a maze and bumping into unfamiliar concepts in the process. But here is the truth God is teaching me:

A wise person *hears*.

It looks simple when written that way, doesn't it? Oh that it were! There are a great many octopus-arms to that statement, and those tentacles reach everywhere. A truly wise person doesn't filter out what he doesn't wish to hear, or filter in only what he wants to hear. He doesn't have "blind spots" or blocks in his hearing. He hears exactly what is communicated.

Now obviously, none of us is perfectly wise. We all are subjective listeners in some instances. We pick up on a certain word, a tone of voice, an expression, or a look, and inflate its importance with preconceived notions, ballooning it out of all proportion. But a wise person will be alert to this danger and ask enough questions to clarify an unclear meaning.

41

I have a dear friend who is very sensitive to me. We had made plans to spend a couple of hours praying together one morning. My day became hectic and I called to tell her I would be late and also would have to leave early from our appointment. Inside I was greatly looking forward to that bright spot of time with the Lord and her, even though it would be shorter than anticipated.

Upon arriving, she told me she wanted to talk about a matter which was difficult to express. Then she said tearfully that she didn't think I really *wanted* to spend time with her and she thought doing so was a burden to me. She loved me enough not to want to be another burden in my already full day.

I wanted to cry and hug her at the same time. She had totally misread me (probably my fault for sounding harried with my interrupted day). But she had the love and wisdom to open up her feelings, and we straightened out the misunderstanding. I shudder to think what would have happened if we had not clarified the situation.

I remember sitting in a booth in Chicago's Museum of Science and Industry twisting small knobs and listening intently to the tiny noise getting higher and higher until I could hear it no longer. The sound was still there, but my ears weren't receiving it. I changed the dial and the machine produced a gradually lowering tone until it registered the lowest sound my ears could hear. I was relieved to find my hearing was in the normal-to-good range and I emerged from the booth smiling.

I only wish my nonphysical hearing mechanism was as healthy!

A while ago I talked with a young wife at a conference. She was downcast as she said, "This has been a wonderful conference but instead of being encouraged, I am feeling utterly defeated. At the tea when the guest speaker shared, I thought, 'I want to be like her, but I never will be. How can I ever hope to be the godly woman that she is?' I feel like giving up and not even trying."

The guest speaker was a friend of mine. In her message she had shared her life in an open, honest way—her defeats and failures as well as her victories. She stated that although she had lost many skirmishes, she knew Christ would win the war. She had readily admitted her shortcomings, but my young companion *had not believed her*. She had not really *heard*, with her heart, all that the speaker was saying. At that point in time, she had become a selective hearer, picking up only a part of what was said and magnifying that part.

I am aware that in many situations, I too hear very partially. And frankly, this scares me. For in hearing only partially, I can hear and interpret my fragmented knowledge 100 percent wrong.

There are reasons for our selective listening. One of the foremost is that we hear with *limited knowledge*.

An irate father phoned the Sunday School superintendent saying that his preschool daughter came home very upset. She had related to him that the Sunday School teacher told the class that if any children missed Sunday School, they would be thrown into the furnace! The superintendent was baffled and called the teacher. The teacher thought and thought about what could have caused this impression, and it finally dawned on her. In order to stress consecutive attendance, she had told her preschool class that if they missed Sunday School four times in a row, they would be dropped from the register!

This little girl had heard with limited knowledge, and so had completely misunderstood what she heard.

A second reason for being a selective hearer is that we hear from a *limited viewpoint*. We are continually filtering information through our own experience, personalities, and backgrounds. My personality is very subjective, so when I hear a friend's heartbreaking tale of a cruel husband I become so emotionally involved that it may be difficult for me to see the husband's side at all. My viewpoint is controlled by my love for my friend and my subjective nature.

A third reason for being a selective hearer is that we listen with *a mind that is already made up*—the "I've made up my mind, don't confuse me with the facts" attitude. In our own eyes, we are right. Yet Solomon warned us that "the way of a fool is right in his own eyes, but a wise man is he who listens to counsel" (Proverbs 12:15).

I listened on an extension the other day, at Jack's request, as he was talking by phone to a close friend of ours who was having a number of problems. Among other things, she was experiencing some physical illness. But the overwhelming ailment she had contracted was a giant case of self-pity. Whenever Jack would remind her that God was still in control, her answer was predictable. "Yes, *but* . . . ." There was such a huge "BUT" between her and the promises of God that she simply could not see God at all. I wondered how many times my own "yes, but" attitude shows that I am approaching a situation with my mind already made up. I often ask for advice only to confirm my own prejudices, and if the adviser doesn't do this, I may dismiss him and look for another counselor.

We had been studying Hebrews 4 in a wives' group the week our friend called. Hebrews 4 portrays the rest we experience in God if we believe and obey Him. But if we are disobedient and unbelieving concerning His promises, our hearts will not be at rest. As I listened to our friend, I thought, "What an example of Hebrews 4! She is not believing in the goodness of God through this. She is full of worry and bitterness, an unhappy, restless person"—which was all true. But right in the middle of thinking this, and despairing that after so many years of such problems she would *never* conquer them, God spoke to *my* heart. He said, "Carole, stop accusing her. What about you? At this moment you are not believing Me either! You are not believing Me for *her* situation. Your heart is not at rest!" God had my attention. I spent some time confessing my unbelief and asking Him to help me overcome.

Wisdom is the ability to hear without filtering out what is unpleasant or disagreeable. Wisdom comes from being wide open, first of all to hear God. "The hearing ear and the seeing eye, the Lord has made both of them" (Proverbs 20:12). Then Scripture says, "Listen, my son, and be wise, and direct your heart in the way" (Proverbs 23:19).

But while we must first be listening to God, true wisdom is also quick to hear men—not just *any* men, but *wise* men. Sometimes we may turn ourselves off to someone whom we have prejudged to be foolish. But these are often poor judgments. Many people are unexpectedly wise. God can make us aware of wise individuals we should consult. "Listen to counsel and accept discipline, that you may be wise the rest of your days" (Proverbs 19:20) and "Incline your ear and hear the words of the wise, and apply your mind to my knowledge . . . that they may be ready on your lips" (Proverbs 22:17-18) are Scriptures we need to think about.

My wisest counselor is Jack. And yet, because my emotions are so tender toward him, it is hard to take correction from him. I have a difficult time being objective about things he suggests. Being aware of this, he is very careful and loving when he tells me something I need to hear. But *because* he loves me, he wants to be faithful to me. "Faithful are the wounds of a friend" (Proverbs 27:6)—and Jack and I are still best friends.

Wisdom is quick to hear reproof—from God, from men, and from life itself. I shy away from reproof. I look at it between half-closed eyes, hoping I don't have to get a complete view of what is wrong with me. But God says, "Do not reprove a scoffer, lest he hate you. Reprove a wise man, and he will love you. Give instruction to a wise man, and he will be still wiser. Teach a righteous man, and he will increase his learning" (Proverbs 9:8-9).

When two people tell us the same thing, when life itself shouts to get our attention, what do we do? Do we block that lesson from our minds? Do we feel like everyone is against us, or that we are being attacked by the enemy?

One passage that recently claimed my attention is Proverbs 15:31-32—"He whose ear listens to the life-giving reproof [or the "reproof of life" in the King James Version] will dwell among the wise. He who neglects discipline despises himself, but he who listens to reproof acquires understanding."

Now I can just hear someone thinking, "But surely Jack is sometimes wrong. And most of the criticism people offer just can't be right. Are *all* reproofs to be taken at face value?"

No. (Aren't you relieved?)

How do you sort them out?

Jack and I have often discussed how blind spots can develop in our lives, and the possibility of getting off course one degree now and ending up 90 degrees off ten years from now. We also discussed how we can prevent this from happening. In our own minds we have decided that if *anyone* reproves us about *anything*, the first thing we need to do is take it to the Lord, thank Him for it, and let Him search our hearts to see if part or all of the criticism is true. If God confirms it, we ask Him to change it in our lives; if not, we ask Him to help us forget it and forgive the one who has unjustly accused us. We have no other option than to patiently accept the criticism in this manner. In 1 Peter 2:20-21 we read, "For what credit is there if, when you sin and are harshly treated, you endure it with patience? But if when you do what is right and suffer for it you patiently endure it, this finds favor with God. For you have been called for this purpose, since Christ also suffered for you, leaving you an example for you to follow in His steps."

This was a difficult passage for me to come to grips with. I could appreciate the fact that I should take patiently the criticism about me that was true, but to accept every unjust criticism patiently? That was tough.

God began to unfold to me however the beautiful reason for this. To take patiently what is true about oneself—any sensible person does that. To take what is untrue with love and forgiveness—now that takes wisdom, focusing our eyes on Christ as our example. For me to be able to accept unjust criticism with the right attitude, God must be the sufficient One in my life. Doing this builds character, and building character is God's work! He has promised to "perfect that which concerneth me" (Psalm 138:8, KJV).

Now if *two* people come to Jack and me about the same thing, the process is the same except we will do even more research and praying. We had better take a good look at ourselves in the light of how people are seeing us, because we are responsible for the impressions we give even if our motives are not at fault.

So Jack and I have concluded that one way to avoid the blind spots we fear is to really *listen* to people. When someone admonishes us we take it to God, thank Him for it, whether it is true or not, and ask Him to sort out the wrong from the right. If there is any truth to it, we ask God to enlighten us concerning it. Whatever is valid, we try to apply. Whatever is not true, we discard and forget, forgiving the person for any hurt received, and *putting it away forever.* "Turn to my reproof, behold, I will pour out my spirit on you; I will make my words known to you" (Proverbs 1:23). We have God's promise that He will make His counsel known to us. He will give us wisdom as we truly listen.

We have God's word on it! It is sufficient.

Lord,
  Open my ears!
  So much that I read in Your Word speaks
    of the importance of hearing.
  Wisdom demands it;
  Righteousness requires it;
  Understanding necessitates it.

I see so much of
  selective hearing.
Am I a selective listener?
Do I only hear what I want to?

Oh, Father!
  You know I long to be
    wise,
    understanding,
    discerning.
  Teach me to hear
    from people
      experiences,
      expressions,

tones from life . . .
With an openness of mind,
a totality of heart,
and an abandonment of my own
preconceived ideas.

Help me to learn.
Teach me to open my ears
and really hear.

Thank You.

6 The Characteristics of Godly Wisdom

"Who among you is wise and understanding?
Let him show by his good behavior his deeds in
  the gentleness of wisdom.
But if you have bitter jealousy and selfish
  ambition in your heart, do not be arrogant
  and so lie against the truth. . . .
The wisdom from above is first pure, then
  peaceable, gentle, reasonable, full of mercy
  and good fruits, unwavering, without
  hypocrisy.
And the seed whose fruit is righteousness is
  sown in peace by those who make peace."

(James 3:13-14, 17-18)

WISDOM FROM ABOVE is pure.

I tried to act nonchalant, as if this were an everyday occurrence. But inside, way down deep where no one can see, I was jumping up and down exclaiming, "Whoopee! Isn't this *something*!"

Jack and I were in Washington, D.C., and having the

privilege of dining with an old friend who was serving in the U.S. Senate. His schedule was tight because the Senate was in session, so he elected to take us to the Senate Dining Room for lunch.

We walked down a long corridor, rode a "Senators only" compartment on the tram between buildings, went up in a "Senators only" elevator, and then were ushered into the Senators' dining room.

I hadn't yet overcome my awe when a petite, pretty woman darted over to our friend and started talking with him. He introduced us to her, and as I was shaking her hand my mind slowly grasped whom I was meeting—Ann Landers!

So there we were in the prestigious Senate Dining Room, Ann Landers and a famous senator at a table immediately behind us, talking with one of the outstanding Christian congressmen of our country. Yes, I was impressed!

Then we were served our food by a smiling black waitress. Our host really didn't need to tell us that the waitress was a sister in Christ—it was evident from her radiant face—but he told us something of her life and how she lived for Christ.

As we sat there having a delicious lunch, I thought, *From man's viewpoint, this is a very prestigious group. One would be hard put to decide who is the wisest person here. But I have a feeling that if we could see from God's viewpoint, this Christian waitress might stand above us all.*

James described godly wisdom as, first of all, *pure*. Why is it *first* of all pure? I think James must have started with this characteristic because in this passage he also describes *natural* wisdom. He tells us that man's natural wisdom is characterized by selfish ambition and bitter jealousy, and that it is earthly and even demonic.

In contrast, God's wisdom is described as having a completely different attitude. Godly wisdom isn't interested in looking out for "number one." It doesn't get jealous when someone else has more success.

The higher one's position, the more jealousy and selfish ambition have to be guarded against. The senators, guests, and even the workers in the Senate Dining Room normally would all have to guard against following natural wisdom very carefully indeed.

God is not impressed by fame, prestige, or intellectual prowess. He looks for purity of heart which is listed first among the characteristics of wisdom. I couldn't help but wonder, that afternoon in the Senate Dining Room, if our smiling waitress would overshadow all the others—in God's sight—for having wisdom that is "first of all pure."

Wisdom from above is also peaceable.

The home in which I grew up was an old, large, colonial-style house. The floors slanted, winds blew in the old windows, and it was drafty and creaky. We loved it! The large, gracious rooms were comforting, and beckoned with open arms the many people who frequented them.

My mother had a heart for the teenagers in our small Michigan town, and as my brother and I began to go to high school she organized and led a teenage Bible study. It grew in numbers to about 30 enthusiastic young people.

During that time, Mother developed a tumor which required serious surgery. She was determined that even while recuperating she would continue with the Bible study group. So she would remain in bed until the group assembled at our home, then put on a hostess gown and come down to teach us. The gown she most frequently wore was one of my favorites. It was white silky material with roses imprinted in a cascade down one side.

For some reason unknown to us, one woman in our town had a hate campaign going against Mother. This woman spread vicious rumors about her continually. The story she made up at this time was that Mother was trying to impress the teenagers by dramatically sweeping downstairs for an "entrance" in a white gown with a sheaf of roses on her arm!

I was furious. I wanted to tell that woman how untrue and unkind her remarks were—and forcefully!

The situation must have concerned Mother as well. But she did something I have never forgotten. She arranged with a local florist to send this lady one red rose every day for a week. Attached to the rose was a card with a verse of Scripture and a note of encouragement.

God used those guileless messages of love and forgiveness to break down a wall of hate. The woman didn't say anything at the time, if I recall correctly, but later on became one of Mother's staunchest supporters.

Wisdom is peaceable. It makes peace. It wins peace.

We don't have too many people around today who are real peacemakers—those who have the kind of godly wisdom it takes to calm troubled seas. Instead, many seem to leave a trail of discontent that can easily be recognized by traces of broken spirits, bitter hearts, and restless souls. Their negativeness is strewn like dusty leaves on the pathways of lives they have touched.

Others pour soothing oil so naturally on places of hurt that a look at the results of their days would reveal they are sowers of peace. The conclusion of their days is summarized in James 3:17: "The seed whose fruit is righteousness is sown in peace by those who make peace."

Wisdom from above is also gentle.

Like purity and peace, gentleness is a fruit of the

Spirit as well as a characteristic of wisdom. (I equate purity with "goodness" in Galatians 5:22-23, where the fruits of the Spirit are listed.) And it certainly takes the Holy Spirit in my life to make me gentle!

The other night I was mentally making a difficult phone call concerning a frustrating situation that had arisen. I projected my imagination in a dozen different versions of "He said . . ." and then "I said . . . ." I was getting angrier all the time, lying there in the darkness as sleep evaded me. (After all, how could I go to sleep in the middle of an argument, even though it was an imaginary one?)

Finally, at 1:30 A.M. I gave up trying and tiptoed into another room, reaching for my Bible. Colossians 3:13-14 grabbed me by the scruff of my argument and shook my anger with a vengeance! "Be gentle and ready to forgive; never hold grudges. Remember, the Lord forgave you, so you must forgive others. Most of all, let love guide your life, for then the whole church will stay together in perfect harmony" (LB).

I made that phone call the next day after asking God to make me wise with His love and gentleness, and to erase all my "vain imaginings." God brought a solution to my frustrations and a peaceful outcome to the problem. His wisdom covered everything.

In myself I have *no* wisdom, and it doesn't seem like I'm getting more in my middle age! The only thing changing is that I'm letting God utilize His wisdom more effectively in my life. I still close Him off at times, but my constant prayer is, "Lord, help me to know You, to be filled full with You so that I will walk in wisdom. I know and believe that You are all-wise."

Colossians 3:16 speaks clearly, "Remember what Christ taught and let His words enrich your lives and make you wise" (LB).

Wisdom from above is also reasonable.

I grew up with one brother, one sister, and a father who was a full-blooded Dutchman. The combination led to great and glorious arguments. We argued when we knew we were wrong. We relished taking the opposite viewpoint on any topic for the sheer delight of the fray. There was no such thing as "giving in." If we were getting verbally mutilated, we simply shouted louder or walked away. To reason quietly, compromise, or conclude an argument never entered our thinking.

Then I married Jack, who claims to be "part Indian and part cowboy" but actually is quiet, reserved English somewhere in his distant past. He is logical and reasonable. Seldom could I entice him into a good argument unless he (1) knew it was important and (2) was correct. How irritating!

But Jack has taught me a great deal about the reasonableness of wisdom, a characteristic which, as the Living Bible says, "allows discussion and is willing to yield to others." Willing to *yield*? Whoever heard of doing *that*?

One of the most helpful things Jack and I have learned in recent years has been the use of the "feedback" technique in communication. This is especially helpful in discussing conflicting ideas. When Jack states his point of view, I say, "If I am hearing you correctly, this is what you are saying . . ." and I repeat what I think he means. He has the opportunity to agree or correct my restatement. He does the same with my opinions. We have found this to be a real asset in clarifying our true understanding of each other. It also helps me see a situation from his point of view rather than only my own. In doing this, we are both willing to yield, compromise, or "agree to disagree" for a time. I am learning that wisdom is *reasonable*. It really does bear up under scrutiny.

Wisdom from above is also full of mercy and good fruits.

Throughout the New Testament we find Christ, who is wisdom, showing abundant mercy and doing good to people. Now that I am a mother-in-law I have taken special note of Peter's concern for his mother-in-law when she was running a high fever (Mark 1:30-31). Finding her ill, Peter, along with his brother and James and John, quickly told Jesus, who immediately did something about the situation. He went to her, took her hand, and healed her. Scripture tells us she then got up and began to serve them.

As I pondered this incident it occurred to me that we often try to reverse the process. Peter's mother-in-law was touched by Christ, healed, and then she served them. We try to serve Him *before* we have been touched by Him—before He has healed us. It seems that we try to heal ourselves by working for Him, instead of waiting for His healing and then serving out of love and gratitude. And we wonder why we aren't more effective in our service!

But Christ understands our frailties, and how we get things backwards sometimes. He is always full of mercy and His mercy is evident in the way He continually ministers to us.

A variety of words are used in different Bible versions for the next attribute of wisdom: "unwavering" (NASB); "without partiality" (KJV); "without uncertainty" (RSV); and "straightforward" (PH). It means that a wise person would follow the right course of action no matter who was involved, and he would be resolute in doing it, knowing it was right. It means hanging on to a decision no matter what adverse winds might blow, and whatever the consequences.

Several years ago we met a man who had just lost his

job as one of the top restaurant managers in Reno, Nevada. Bill related to us that a year or so previously he hired a young, outgoing Christian to help him manage one of the several restaurants for which he was responsible. It wasn't long before a number of the college students who worked there began meeting regularly for Bible study, and stopped spending their wages on the slot machines. Bill was himself a "secret" Christian and was challenged by these students. He began attending one of the Bible studies and started growing spiritually. Soon he became active in winning other workers to Christ and helping them in their walk with Christ.

After a few months, the owner of the restaurants, which were connected to gambling establishments which he also owned, called Bill into his office to talk about his "religious activities." It seemed that they were hurting his gambling business! Finally the owner gave Bill an ultimatum: either quit his religious activities or lose his job. Bill resigned on the spot.

Bill was telling a group of young people about this a short time later when one of them asked incredulously, "You mean you gave up your job?"

Bill smiled and said, "Of course I gave up my job! Men give their *lives* for this!"

Bill was unwavering in his stand—without partiality in his witness. He paid a price, but he will have a far greater reward.

The best piece of advice I ever heard a mother give was offered by a woman in my hometown who had three very active boys—the best behaved boys around. When asked the secret of her success she said, "I never say no unless I have to. But when I have to, I never make an exception. I mean it." She was an unusual mother, and one whose wisdom was unwavering.

Wisdom from above is also without hypocrisy.

Who comes immediately to your mind when the quality of being without hypocrisy is mentioned? Who is the example you would use of a sincere, guileless person? One who epitomizes this characteristic to me is Lorne Sanny, the president of The Navigators.

Twenty-some years ago when Jack and I first joined the staff of The Navigators, we lived in a small log cabin just outside the gates of Glen Eyrie, the Navigator headquarters in Colorado Springs. Jack helped with conferences and managed the print shop, a job he really didn't know much about. Today Jack has the privilege of working closely with Lorne.

Mr. Sanny's attitude toward me has been exactly the same throughout the years. He has been gracious, kind, and friendly. To me, he is the embodiment of a sincere man, without a shred of hypocrisy in his makeup, and I appreciate this quality in him.

* * * *

In the light of these qualities of godly wisdom, is it any wonder that James asked the searching question "Who among you is wise and understanding?" (James 3:13)? His subsequent statement is profound: "Let him show [demonstrate] by his good behavior his deeds in the gentleness of wisdom." The qualities of wisdom are not in words, but in actions. They are seen in our behavior and our deeds, and the sum of them is "the gentleness of wisdom."

Lord, thank You for showing me
  what wisdom is
  and what it does.
Please, keep teaching me.
Don't stop now.

7 The Results of Wisdom

IT WAS A SPARKLING DAY in Colorado. Driving toward the mountains, I thought, *Lord, I can't even imagine heaven being more beautiful than this. What a Creator You are!*

On my way home from running my errand, again I observed God's handiwork and thought how wonderful it would be to go Home . . . to be with God in a twinkling. I said, "Lord, I'd like to just go Home right now. I guess lots of people long for heaven when things are really bad, but somehow right now, in the beauty of this moment, I long to go to heaven just so I can see more of You, and get to know You better."

Within my heart, God answered with a thought I'd never considered before. He said, "Carole, you will never get to know Me in heaven in the way you are getting to know Me *right here*."

As I pondered this, I suddenly realized what He was saying. We get to know God through suffering here. There will be no suffering there. We learn how to see God through tears, feel His comfort in pain, and hear His voice of strength in trials and tribulations. There will be no tears, no pain, no trials, no tribulation there. So in these very precious ways, we know God *better* down here. We are learning things about Him we could never discover in heaven! And we can take that knowledge with us when we go to be with Him forever.

No wonder we are to welcome trials as friends. No wonder we are to count it all joy to suffer!

I'm sure God smiled when, after getting really excited about this wonderful truth, I had to tell Him, "That's exciting, Father. But I still don't think I'll ask for more pain, if You don't mind. I want to get to know You more than, well, most anything . . . but I'm still a coward. Still, send me what You know is best for me."

I know He will.

I believe God gave me a bit of wisdom that day—insight into His plan and purpose for the pain in my life. Glimpses of truth from God can be one way to gauge whether we are open to His wisdom. Is He teaching us new and precious truths about Himself each day, each week? God is such a many-splendored Person that we will never come to the end of learning fresh lessons about His character. If we aren't, it isn't God's fault. It is ours for not opening ourselves to His teaching.

I began to think about other tangible signs of wisdom—God's wisdom—in our lives, and realized that we find some measuring sticks in the Bible that help us know whether we are being open to Him.

One question we might ask ourselves is "Who am I close to?" Who is influencing us? What voice or voices are we taking careful note of? When Jack and I asked a member of Congress what kind of leader a newly elected president would make, his wise reply was, "I'm waiting to find out what kind of men he will gather around him."

Solomon, the wisest king of all history, declared, "A wise man will hear and increase in learning, and a man of understanding will acquire wise counsel" (Proverbs 1:5).

Not only will a wise man seek qualified counselors, but he will also carefully select his friends and companions as well. God warns us that "he who walks with wise men will be wise, but the companion of fools will suffer harm" (Proverbs 13:20).

In a great many instances we allow ourselves to be influenced wrongly. Often, very subtly and without thinking, we listen to the clamoring voices around us, and buy whatever philosophy the world is selling today. Our minds are deluged with a flood of worldly ideas, and we may drown without a struggle, not realizing we have been easy victims.

When Joye was first in the hospital with leukemia, God gave her the ability to accept her illness and she had the opportunity to witness to a number of the hospital personnel. After she returned home, we heard from one of the Christian workers in the hospital that the nurses felt Joye had not accepted her situation—that she was not facing the fact that she was terminally ill. As we examined why they should think that, we realized it was because she had not gone through the "five stages of dying." Some experts tell us that everyone faced with death goes through five phases: shock and rejection, anger, bargaining, depression, and finally acceptance. Joye immediately moved into stage five and the nurses did not understand it.

Now I am not saying Christians never go through those five stages. But I am saying they don't necessarily have to. We often accept such a concept from the world's point of view without holding it up to the standard of God's Word.

Another concept we have bought from the world concerns expressing our anger. We are told that it is not healthy to repress our emotions, that we must let them all hang out. But Scripture tells us we are to be slow to anger, to be cool in our spirits, to think before we speak. We do have to get it out, but we can get it out to *God* and let Him handle our feelings, erase our anger, or help us manage that anger with wisdom which is pure and gentle.

Our standards of purity are being subjected to a not-so-quiet brainwashing process by television, books, movies, magazines, and newspapers. But we are warned, "Don't let the world around you squeeze you into its own mold" (Romans 12:2, PH).

One of the ways to combat this constant pressure is to ask God to surround us with wise people as our counselors, friends, and companions—individuals who will sharpen us, challenge us, and instruct us. They should be friends whose eyes are on the Lord and who will help us keep our eyes on Him too.

Another measure of a wise person is that he will have a life marked by discipline and obedience. "Whoso keepeth the law is a wise son" (Proverbs 28:7, KJV). Jesus said, "Every one who hears these words of Mine, and acts upon them, may be compared to a wise man, who built his house upon a rock" (Matthew 7:24).

Finally, the *behavior* of a wise person will make his understanding apparent. It will be good behavior. He won't lie (Proverbs 24:28) or be lazy (Proverbs 24:30-34). He won't say that wrong is right (Proverbs 24:24) or show partiality (Proverbs 24:23). His tongue will bring healing (Proverbs 12:18) and will make knowledge acceptable (Proverbs 15:2). He will learn by observation (Proverbs 24:32).

How amazing are wisdom's results! In Proverbs 24:13-14 we are told that wisdom is sweet like honey to the soul. "If you find it, then there will be a future, and your hope will not be cut off."

As I have written these chapters I have realized that only a fraction of the tip of an iceberg is showing. God's wisdom—the kind He wants to give me—is a concept I trust will be growing in me for the rest of my life.

But the twofold aspect of my first feeble prayer is crystal-clear now. The request in the first part of Psalm 90:12—"Teach us to number our days"—puts the responsibility squarely on God to teach me as I ask Him. It is His promise to train me in wisdom. The second part of the verse, "that we may present to Thee a heart of wisdom," pointedly shows me my duty to listen, to be open to His light, to search my heart, and then to present, or, as the King James Version translates, to "apply" my heart to wisdom.

With these shining truths radiating around me, I look to heaven and say, "Thank You, Father. What next?"

PART TWO
Wisdom for a Wife

8 Called by God

IT WAS A TELEPHONE SURVEY, and I was hastily answering the caller's persistent questions.

"And what do you do?" she asked.

I hesitated, then said, "I'm a writer."

After hanging up the phone, I was struck with the "what" and "why" of my answer. True, I had written one slim volume which had just been published. But being a writer was an avocation, not my vocation. I do lots of things—drive a car, cook, lead Bible studies, clean house, speak, counsel people. But my *vocation* is to be a *wife*. Jack's wife. This is my call from God. It is my primary ministry.

I work at my vocation primarily in a house. That makes me a housewife.

The new daughter-in-law of a friend of mine observed after a meeting of wives that when introducing themselves, each wife identified herself by her husband's job.

This young wife was afraid that we women were losing our identity as persons, and I nodded assent. Perhaps, I thought, we have been "wife brainwashed."

But as I reflected later, it gradually dawned on me that it wasn't the women at that meeting who had been brainwashed, but my friend's young daughter-in-law.

When men are introducing themselves, they usually tell what they do: "I am John Jones, sales manager of Marathon." Am I to say that I am Carole Mayhall, person? Writer? Sanguine? New learner of tennis? No, I identify myself with my call from God—my main purpose in my ministry. I am Carole Mayhall, housewife—called to be Jack's wife, in our house. I have been working at this job for 27 years now, and it truly is my vocation.

Why have I let myself be bullied into being ashamed of God's primary call as though it were insignificant and not worthy of my life? I have avoided calling myself "housewife" as if it were a dirty word. I have referred instead to my occupation as "homemaker" and, recently, "writer."

One meaning of the Hebrew word for "woman" is "a helper as man's counterpart." I am Jack's counterpart, completing him and helping him be what God wants him to be. And this frees me to be all God wants me to be as well. Thank God, He has let me be a housewife!

To be a wife is an adventure! As I was contemplating this concept I began to see how much wisdom I need for my adventure-vocation. A verse rang an alarm bell in my mind: "The wise woman builds her house, but the foolish tears it down with her own hands" (Proverbs 14:1). God had begun to give me a glimpse of what wisdom *was*, and now He was telling me what to do with it. I am to build my house. But what comprises my "house"? I concluded that a woman's house consists of the people in her sphere of influence. Every woman builds or tears down. No neutral ground is possible. In my mind I paraphrased that verse, "A wise woman builds into the lives of those around her, but a foolish woman tears down others' lives." This brought my thinking to the one closest to me—my husband. I was to build up my husband, not tear him down. And this building is a many-faceted task.

The question I often ask women who are contemplating marriage is, "Do you feel you are *called by God* to be the wife of this man?" Marriage should not be something one drifts into or decides to do in order to get out of something else. It should be as surely a call from God as is a call to the mission field, or to full-time Christian service. And it is a unique call.

The last part of Romans 8:28 tells us we are *called* according to God's purpose. We are assured that God leads us in the way we should go (Isaiah 48:17) and will guide us with His counsel (Psalm 73:24). His holy calling for us is "not according to our works, but according to *His own purpose* and grace which was granted us in Christ Jesus from all eternity" (2 Timothy 1:9). Therefore if He has led us and guided us to be married, we are called to that specific plan of His for our lives.

If we realize deep within our hearts that our marriage is a call from God, our attitudes change. If we view marriage as just another job and just another situation, then when things get rough we begin to complain, and some start to think of ways to get out.

If we knew beyond all doubt we had a call to the mission field, and then began to experience persecution or saw few results for our labors, we would still believe it was God's overall plan for us. We would try not to doubt what God had called us to do. Something of the same is true in our marriages. When we know it is God's call for us to be a wife, our perspective alters. When things become difficult, we can believe it is part of God's plan to perfect us, to help us know Him, to strengthen us to work through the difficulties, and to be fruitful for Him.

When I am assured that God's call for me is to be a wife, I can begin with assurance to discover what that ministry includes. I can ask a creative God for creative ideas to develop my ministry, and so *build* into the life of my husband.

> *Oh, Father . . .*
> *You have given me a glimpse*
> *of what wisdom is,*
> *and now one small insight*
> *into what it does.*
> *Thank You.*
> *Now I need Your help*
> *to know HOW to build.*
> *Teach me, please.*

9 Her Husband's Crown

"AN EXCELLENT WIFE is the crown of her husband . . . ." (Proverbs 12:4). I puzzled over those words. *How can a wife be a crown to her husband?* I thought. I could understand the rest of the verse—"but she who shames him is as rottenness in his bones." But the thought of being a crown wasn't at all clear to me.

Should a wife make her husband feel like royalty? Perhaps. But I felt there was a deeper meaning. As I pondered, it occurred to me that a crown symbolizes many things, but one primary consideration is that a crown sets someone apart as being *very special*.

It was a beautiful evening, and another wife and I were sharing it on the lakeshore. The moon's reflection shimmered in the water around the dock. When I commented on the beauty of the moment, her response was, "Yes, but my husband would never notice."

Into my mind popped the image of a grim-faced, unromantic clod! And I didn't even know her husband!

How many times have slighting remarks about our husbands cast them in a negative light—remarks such as

"Jim was really in a horrible mood this morning"; "He's a stickler for our budget until *he* decides to buy something"; "He never remembers my birthday." Instead of setting them apart with respect and honor, our words portray our husbands as individuals with glaring faults.

In *Beyond the Male Myth*, authors Dr. Anthony Pietropinto and Jacqueline Simenauer report they interviewed 4,000 men and discovered some interesting facts. Given a list of qualities to be desired most in a steady sex partner, the men checked "A woman with a concern for my needs" 28.4 percent of the time; "A sincere woman" 23 percent; "An affectionate woman" 20.8 percent; "An intelligent woman" 16.1 percent; "A self-confident woman"12.2 percent; "A sexy woman" 11.1 percent; and "A woman with a good sense of humor" 10.3 percent.[1]

It is interesting that the men most often checked "A woman with a concern for my needs." If we have a concern for the needs of our husbands, we will recognize that one of their greatest needs is for us to think of them as unique and remarkable. And we must be willing to let our husbands—and the world—know how we feel.

"A national sales executive came to New York City and put an ad in the paper with an offer to twenty men who would meet his qualifications. He offered $35,000 a year for five years plus $250,000 to a million dollars to start their own businesses. He opened shop in a motel room for three weeks, interviewing men for eighteen hours a day. At the end of three weeks he had his twenty men.

"He then did a very unusual thing. He asked to interview the wives of the twenty men. One by one the women came, and after talking with all twenty women, he had only nine men left. He said he did not interview the women to determine their intelligence, their beauty, or their poise. He interviewed each woman to see if she was on her husband's team and would stand behind him. He said he was offering the men a great opportunity, but one which would require hard work and dedication. He knew that without the encouragement and praise of their wives the men would not succeed. Would your husband have been one of the nine men left?"[2]

A few years ago Jack spoke at a conference, and after he had finished a man came up to me and said, "It must be wonderful to be married to a man like that."

I said, "You better believe it is. Next to knowing Christ as my Savior, it's the most wonderful thing in the world."

I will never forget the look of longing that crossed this man's face as he said wistfully, "Oh, I hope my wife feels like that."

I thought, *Oh friend, your wife should let you* know *this is how she feels, for she has been commanded to be a crown to her husband.*

This is not optional. If we are to be an excellent wife (and I know we long to be that), we *will be* a crown to our husbands. If we are not a crown, we may well be "as rottenness in his bones." I see no alternatives to these two choices. A wife either makes her husband know he is distinct and important, or she "corrodes his strength and tears down everything he does" (Proverbs 12:4, LB). Our husbands desperately need our affirmation. We can affirm him in our communication with him, and by how we represent him to other people.

Listening to the car radio as I drove toward Pikes Peak one afternoon, the words of a song caught my attention. It was a haunting tale sung by a man to the girl he loved, telling her he would love her now and tell her lies to try to make her happy, but he knew sooner or later he would leave her because he had feet of sand. Then these words:

"Someday I'll leave you behind
Because love is just a state of mind."

I wanted to shout, "*No*! No, that isn't true! Love is an act of the will which may or may not be accompanied by "a state of mind."

Last week one of my friends told me her husband came home and said, "I'm not sure I love you anymore. I don't have any feeling for you. I don't even feel like coming home."

This attitude is a result of the world's view of love. In our Hollywood-Playboy world, love is a feeling that fluctuates with the moods of the moment. But real love is so much more than that. Love is commitment—to God and to a person. It is a commitment of our *wills*. It is an attitude that states, "I will love you with a love that is patient and kind" and all the other wonderful ingredients that 1 Corinthians 13 talks about. It is a commitment that says, "I will give you love when I feel like it, when I don't feel like it, and until I do feel like it."

Early last December Jack came in with a beautifully wrapped package which he said I could open right away. Inside, nestled among layers of white paper, was one of the most beautiful Christmas centerpieces I have ever seen—three large red candles surrounded by greens and holly. I was delighted. As I kissed him and expressed my appreciation I asked, "Hey, what's the occasion?" His reply was classic: "Well," he said, "I wasn't feeling very loving today so I decided to do a loving act." (Due to some pressures at work, he had been absorbed with everything but me.) Later he told me that picking out something he knew would delight me made a greater *feeling* of love flow back into his life.

Jack and I broke our engagement three times before we finally understood the difference between real love and a loving feeling. When pressures of school would get to us and block some of the feelings we had about each other, we mistakenly thought our love was gone.

I would have a hard time without experiencing the feeling of love over any length of time. Being a feeling-oriented person, it would be very difficult if I didn't *feel* "in love" with Jack. But there are many kinds of love—the love of friendship, respect, sharing deep experiences together, the love that is based on the knowledge that God has led you together, love that feels protective, and of course the feeling-oriented physical or sexual love. If I base my "I love you" only on the latter, then when my husband has the flu, when pressures build to an exploding point, when long absences occur, when tempers are short, and in a hundred other situations, my "love" may fade. There are times in every couple's life when the thought pops into mind, "I don't like you!" Actually, if one analyzed it, it probably would really be "I don't like something you did." But at that point, who is analyzing? And because liking and loving are so integrally entwined, the feeling of love suddenly disappears and one is left wondering what happened.

When a commitment to love is an act of our wills, even the wondering becomes less and less frequent. Whether you feel loving or not stops entering into the thinking process after living years together knowing God wants you *committed* to love. For a married Christian woman, part of demonstrating her love is being a crown to her husband.

I remember hearing a man say, "He seems like an ordinary fellow but he must have something on the ball. You should see the kind of woman he married!" When the "ordinary" man was examined more closely, it was found that, indeed, he was exceptional—something that may never have surfaced but for its reflection in the heart of his wife.

In Proverbs 31 we find God's portrayal of a godly wife whose husband is "known in the gates," meaning that her husband was respected and well thought of in the community *because of her.*

Question: Are our husbands "known in the gates," by people they have never met, because our lives reflect favorably on them?

Every once in a while I am introduced to a person whom Jack has met and talked with during a trip. It is thrilling to me when that person says, "After hearing Jack talk about you, I could hardly wait to meet you!" Can you imagine what that does to me? Well, I want to be every bit as much a champion for my husband as he is for me. I want to set him apart as being someone special (because he is!) to those to whom I am his only representative. But I also want him to know—in every way possible—that to me, he is one "set apart from the others." I want to be a "crown" to Jack and to build him up in this way.

Father, help me be Jack's "crown." Give me a conviction of my call from You. And please keep teaching me how to build.
Thank You.

---

1. Anthony Pietropinto, M.D., and Jacqueline Simenauer, *Beyond the Male Myth* (New York: Times Books, 1977). page 243. © 1977 by Anthony Pietropinto.
2. Linda Dillow, *Creative Counterpart* (Nashville and New York: Thomas Nelson, Inc., 1977), pages 92-93.

10 Growing with Him

RAINDROPS SPLATTERED on our windshield. Except for the accompanying purr of the engine, they provided the only sound in our car. I was thinking of the conversation Jack had just related.

During a recent five-hour flight across the United States, Jack asked his seat companion, "What is the purpose of your move to California?"

A wry smile refused to reach her eyes as the young woman responded, "A good marriage gone bad."

She poured out a familiar story to his sympathetic ear. She worked after her marriage to put her husband through law school. Now that he was a successful lawyer he had met someone more his equal intellectually, although this other woman wasn't physically attractive, according to the young wife. Now the husband was divorcing her to marry someone else for intellectual reasons.

It comes in all guises: One partner simply outgrows the other . . . or they think they do.

In graduate school we lived in a 28-foot trailer parked in "Trailerville," with about 40 others, on the school's grounds. One wife near us helped her husband through college and seminary and raised three children in the process. She completed only high school before stopping her formal schooling. The seminary did not offer courses at that time for wives. So I often wondered if she was able to talk to her husband about the complicated studies he was pursuing.

Because Jack and I did not have children in our school days, our trailer was often the gathering place for some of the men to discuss deep theological and philosophical issues. Even when I went to bed before their conversations ended, I could not fail to hear them through the thin door separating our bedroom from the living room. I listened whether I wanted to or not!

We could not afford to pay someone to type Jack's term papers or his thesis. As poor as I am at typing, I am a little better than he is. So many evenings were spent typing his projects and thereby learning something about the subjects he was studying. As we discussed those issues I kept up with some of the courses he was taking. Looking back, I am grateful to God for forcing me to learn along with Jack.

What can a wife do to grow with her husband? Let me suggest some do's and don'ts for building into the life of one's husband. These suggestions are intended to help you develop your mind, and so stay in his intellectual ballpark.

DON'T:

1. Watch daytime television. There isn't much intellectual stimulation in the daily suds of the soap operas. Most husbands are not turned on by a recital of the events in the characters' lives.

2. Read only women's journals, romantic novels, and comics.

3. Concentrate only on so-called "feminine hob-

bies," such as needlepoint, crafts, and plants. Now notice I said *only*. These are all great—and any hobby will help make you a more interesting person, but people can be quickly bored by hearing how wall hangings are made.

DO:

1. Read, read, read—*Reader's Digest, U.S. News and World Report* (and other news magazines), travel books, biographies, and other books about a variety of subjects. But especially make it a goal to read a book every year in your husband's field. So your husband is an ontologist and you can't spell it, let alone understand it? Then ask him for a beginning book, and he'll be charmed by your interest! At least you may glean enough knowledge to become an intelligent listener, and to ask a good question or two now and then.

2. Continue your education. Never, never stop learning. I am not necessarily talking about taking an extension course from your local college, or even a correspondence course, although both are excellent ideas (and some correspondence courses let you go at your own pace without pressure to complete them in a specified length of time). Many mini-courses are also available through churches, park and recreation departments, and health services. There is no excuse for us to stop learning. I phoned the public library today, and found they lend Spanish records. We are planning a trip to Mexico next year and I would very much like to recover some of my college-level Spanish.

There are courses in most cities on heart massage and first aid, crafts and sports, interpersonal relationships, Church history, or an Old Testament survey. The lists go on and on.

But you may need an even more ambitious program. One friend of mine, whose husband has a Ph.D., finished college and started a master's program as an active wife and the mother of four children. She is growing right along with her husband, and recently co-authored a book with him. To her I say, "Right on!"

Now not all of us are our husband's intellectual equals, and that's okay too. But to give up, to immerse ourselves in soap operas and the world of our children, and not to begin awakening the billions of brain cells we possess—this is very sad. Part of the privilege of being a wife, of being a true helper for your husband, is growing *with* him. He will appreciate your efforts, and you will be a more interesting person not just to him, but to yourself and others as well.

There may be a question here from wives whose husbands are not growing—men who run on only one track, such as the business track. Wouldn't a growing wife be threatening? Couldn't this cause problems?

This situation calls for unique wisdom. The wife needs to keep growing because God has told her to "grow in the grace and knowledge of our Lord and Savior Jesus Christ" (2 Peter 3:18), for her own self-worth, and to be a challenge to her husband. But she will need to ask for true humility not to flaunt her growth or feel superior, for grace not to push her husband to "get going," and for great love to accept her husband just the way he is. She will have to be a subtle grower. But grow she must, or she will die inside.

3. Delve into new topics. Explore new horizons. Ask God for new challenges.

Have you ever prayed that God would teach you a new thing about Himself every week, and that He would identify the characteristic for you in a concrete way?

Have you ever prayed that God would give you a new interest each month? It can be something that is not too time-consuming (you may have more than you can handle already), but something fun to do and interesting to talk about—something *not* in your husband's field of interest, or that he necessarily cares to know about, but something that will make you grow and expand your mind.

4. Develop interesting friends—or perhaps I should say develop friends who have interests that differ from yours. Encourage them to talk about those subjects. Learn to ask questions as if you were drawing water from a deep well (see Proverbs 20:5).

5. Snatch every opportunity to learn. Watch a news documentary instead of a game show. Stay and talk a few moments to the missionary who spoke at church, and ask some penetrating questions. Ask your neighbor about her favorite hobby.

6. Ask our creative God for creative ideas as to how you can grow with your husband. Ask your husband for his ideas. Ask everybody!

God made you to be a creative counterpart. He wants the two of you to be far more as a couple than both of you could be alone. He would not have a husband outgrow his wife or grow so lazy in mind and heart that no stretching and learning takes place. How could two, so far apart, be really "one"?

So stretch your mind and let God give you ideas for becoming a deeper, more thoughtful individual—one who will sharpen, challenge, excite, expand, and delight others.

Grow.

Father, God,
How can we thank You
for the laughter shared
the tears shed
the pain felt
the joy experienced

the times of ecstasy
  and disappointment
  and blessings
  and trials?
You've used them all, Lord,
  to help us see Your face more clearly
  and feel a closeness
  with each other that is
  precious and glowing.
Don't stop, please.
Keep us growing,
  conformed to Your image
  ever deeper in our love.
Help us walk in love
  hand in hand
  with each other
  and with You.
May we walk in wisdom,
  Your gentle
    reasonable
    peaceful
    wisdom.
May we walk in Your Spirit,
  controlled and filled
  full with God Himself.
Help us plumb depths we don't know exist
  to reach for heights we aren't aware of.
Keep us loving . . . and loved.

                                    Thank You

11 Knowing Him

I<small>T WAS A FREEWHEELING</small> DISCUSSION among eight wives, touching on a wide variety of topics and eventually turning to the importance of knowing one's husband. Jan, a slender brunette with a gracious manner, came up with the prize idea of the afternoon.

"Bob and I are very different in a number of ways," she explained, "but especially in the way we handle an issue about which we disagree. Bob loves to get in the ring and spar. I will go to almost any lengths to avoid any kind of fight.

"One day it occurred to me that when Bob was interacting with certain friends, he came home excited and stimulated. But with other people he would come home worn out and disheartened. I began to wonder if there was a pattern in the kind of people who stimulated him. So I determined to study those who inspired and sharpened him, and also those who left him deadened and dampened in spirit. To my astonishment I soon found the common denominator of the first group was that they took unabashed issue with his thinking. They challenged him, and made him think more keenly. Being a very objective person this did not threaten or upset him. The latter kind of people simply agreed with everything he thought, and drained him.

"So as I prayed about being the kind of wife I wanted to be for him, I asked the Lord for the courage—because in my case that was what it took—to 'put on my boxing gloves and get in the ring.' The next time Bob came up with an idea I didn't buy, I took a deep breath and said, 'I disagree with that 100 percent!' Immediately we were really going at it verbally. As we were clashing verbal swords and the sparks were flying, inside I was cringing. Suddenly Bob threw back his head and laughed. He said, 'Man this is great! Why don't we do this more often?'"

Jan is one wise woman.

Proverbs says, "Iron sharpens iron, so one man sharpens another" (27:17). God may want you to be a sharpening agent in the life of your husband—not to cut him down or make him bleed, but to hone the fine edges of his mind.

Often we hear how important it is to study the man God has given to us, but we are not told how to do it. Jan had hit on a way I never thought of until that moment. But she hadn't stopped with just finding out the kind of people who stimulated her husband. She had prayed for the ability to *be* that kind of person for Bob. She will grow more and more into the kind of woman who truly satisfies her husband's needs.

In order to build into the lives of our husbands, we have to know them. And knowing them, truly knowing them, will take years of study. They are constantly changing, as we are, so this task will never be finished. But what rewarding work—work that has lasting rewards! God will give us understanding to ensure success.

One of the first things to learn in order to study one's husband is the art of questioning—learning to ask questions which are interesting for him to answer, informative to you, deep in quality, and nonthreatening. Let me give you seven questions[1] as a test to see how well you know your husband. Some of them might be used as a springboard for some interesting conversation on your "dates."

"1. What is the happiest thing that has ever happened to your husband?
2. What has been the hardest experience of his life?
3. What are his secret ambitions, his goals for his life?
4. What are his deep fears?
5. What about you does he appreciate the most?
6. What traits of yours would he like to see changed?
7. What man or men does he most admire?"

When reading a book, write down in a notebook interesting thoughts or questions to stimulate conversation. Ask other wives for good questions. Take a course in family counseling or read a book on counseling to gather ideas on ways to break through the armor of silence.

Pray. Ask our inventive God for ideas to build bridges across the silent stream between the two of you. Build new avenues to travel together. Ask your husband for his schedule as the day begins: appointments, meetings, and important decisions that need to be made. As you pray through your day, pray through his day as well. You will find yourself more involved in your husband's life, and with more knowledgeable questions to ask him.

Second, study his habits and his work. Is he a prompt person, or is he habitually late? Is he a morning, afternoon, or evening person? Neat or casual? Does he dream at night? Daydream? Fantasize? If so, about what? Is he disciplined? In what areas? What about his work bores him, stimulates him, or disturbs him?

Ask yourself a hundred questions, and then study him to find the answers. Know him. Find out what makes him angry, bored, slightly irritated, amused, or discouraged. Study him!

One Sunday evening in January Jack and I were returning from a trip when we were stranded in the Dallas airport in four-degree weather. The unusual cold caused havoc at the airport. The trams weren't running, the terminal was freezing, the electric clocks were spinning wildly. I had a splitting headache and was dead tired as we waited in the cold for a bus to transfer us from one terminal to another.

My reaction to a situation like this is forced cheerfulness. I refuse to let dismal circumstances take over, so I compel myself to have a cheery attitude, try to make a joke out of the difficulties, and become helpful to older ladies around me. The truth is, I also become obsessively talkative and "hyper." So that evening as we were standing among a crowd of irritated people, I was excessively talkative, assuring an infrequent traveler that "all the planes must be running late, I'm sure you will make yours" and on and on. At that point I felt the pressure of Jack's hand on my thigh. It was his way of saying, "Carole, you are talking too much. Please cool it!"

That's all it took! I "cooled it." I didn't talk for the rest of the trip. Two minutes after he had communicated in that nonverbal way, he said, "I'm sorry, honey. I wasn't accepting you. Please forgive me." But by that time, it was too late. My headache and DRA (dirty rotten attitude) had completely taken over. When we arrived home at 2:00 A.M. we both said we were sorry again and went to bed. I was no longer angry. I was too wiped out to be feeling *anything*.

The next morning I was tempted to forget the whole incident. But then I realized it provided an opportunity to learn more about one another in an area never before explored. First I had to pray and ask God for wisdom to understand myself. Why do I feel I need to force cheerfulness in a bad situation? (Answer: I don't know, but the realization came that this has been my reaction since my teens.) Second, I had to ask God to help me to think through Jack's usual reaction to a rough situation. I realized that he withdraws and is increasingly more silent, continuing to be helpful to me but just sort of "bearing it"—an exactly opposite response to my hyper-helpful activity. No wonder it irritated him! It would have irritated Saint Paul himself.

As we discussed it over a cup of coffee, I told him what I had realized, and asked, "I really will try not to be so talkative in a situation like last night. But if I can't, would you rather I am totally silent or like I was at the airport?" He replied that he wanted me to be me (bless him!).

We had broken through to some better understanding that morning. I had never analyzed his reaction to discomforting situations, and so now I understood him better. As I comprehended his silence, I could understand more completely his irritation at my chatter. It was something for us to pray about and consider.

A third thing to study is the people your husband likes and who challenge him—as Jan did with her husband. Try to figure out common traits in these people that appeal to your husband. Then ask God to mold you and help you grow in these characteristics.

Fourth, study articles and books that give help in understanding people in general and your husband in particular. A book that turned on some lights of understanding for me was Tim LaHaye's *Spirit Controlled Tempera-*

ment. It gave insight into the fact that Jack (choleric-phlegmatic) and I (mostly sanguine) approach things from very different frameworks. Reading Paul Tournier's *To Understand Each Other* was also enlightening regarding personality differences. Magazine and newspaper articles, if one sorts through them intelligently, can also be a source of good information. Did you ever become irritated that your husband seemed to be in a steak-and-potato rut when you dine out? According to Dr. Joyce Brothers this is very common for most men. She says that when dining out, men order the same old standbys and women tend to try exotic foods. Men are not as adventurous. She also relates that most arguments are started by wives—in nine out of eleven instances in fact. Males are disinclined to fight the female of the species and have a feeling of forbearance toward them. She tells us that women are more subject to being depressed and to worrying more about themselves and about their men; that they are less likely to go to pieces in trying situations than men, perhaps not in inconsequential matters but in matters of life or death; and that women have more nightmares, require appreciably more sleep, and have more colds than men.[2] These are interesting observations to help us understand ourselves as well as those creatures we married.

Do you ever take "marriage success" tests in magazines? Some may be inaccurate, but often they bring a glimmer of understanding. At best they can be helpful, and at worst they might provide a good laugh! One recent gem by Mary Susan Miller in *Family Weekly*[3] reported that men and women enter marriage expecting very different things. And unless this is understood, trouble can and will result. She reports that Dr. Clifford Adams of Pennsylvania State University devised a test for married couples listing six ingredients of marriage, and asked 6,000 couples to rank them individually in order of importance. The results showed how differently husbands and wives rated these ingredients:

MEN	WOMEN
1. Companionship	1. Love and affection
2. Sex	2. Security
3. Love and affection	3. Companionship
4. Home and family	4. Home and family
5. Encouraging helpmate	5. Encouraging helpmate
6. Security	6. Sex

The couples were also asked to list the six ingredients in the order they thought their spouse would rank them. Husbands listed "Home and family" as their wives' top choice, while the wives listed "Sex" for their husbands.

Dr. Selma Miller, president of the Association of Marriage and Family Counselors, was quoted in the same article. "The most common cause of marriage problems," she said, "is that partners' needs are in conflict, but they can't discuss the conflict because they don't know one exists. They only know they are miserable."

What this could be saying to us—if we fall into a "typical" category—is that the man may spend years trying to force his wife to be a buddy and pal, while the woman may spend years trying to force her husband to be a father figure and to treat her as her father had done years before. So we need wisdom not only to know where our husband is coming from, what he is looking for in our marriage and in us, but also wisdom to know what we really need from our relationship. It is a complicated process that takes much study and prayer for wisdom.

I have touched only the surface of some of the ways we can study and know our husbands. To go on might be futile at any rate, since all of us are so different. But why don't you take a little time right now to commit this whole matter to our heavenly Father? Ask Him for wisdom, understanding, insight, and a knowledge of your husband's personality, needs, and thinking. Ask God for a lifelong desire to grow daily in understanding, and to keep you aware of the exciting adventure of discovery—the discovery of intimately knowing another person created in the image of God.

1. Linda Dillow, *Creative Counterpart*, page 95.
2. Dr. Joyce Brothers, "Oldest Miracle Is Love," the *Colorado Springs Gazette Telegraph* (Knight News Service), March 15, 1977, page 9A.
3. Mary Susan Miller, "Do Men and Women Expect the Same Things From Marriage?" *Family Weekly*, May 8, 1977, page 18.

12 Appreciating Him

"**I**F I HEAR IT ONE MORE TIME, I'm going to vomit" she exclaimed. I could certainly sympathize. We women have been written to, spoken to, urged, and exhorted to encourage, admire, appreciate, and accept our husbands. We are weary with the hearing.

And the most exasperating thing of all is that what we are told is true!

Many good ideas have been written concerning building into the life of your husband by appreciating and admiring him, but let's look at it from a slightly different angle.

Several years ago when money for extras in our household was almost nonexistent, I was given a secondhand beige winter coat by my mother-in-law. I was grateful for the coat but beige makes me look like cold toast, so I spent seven precious dollars having that coat dyed a bright blue.

One day I was downtown wearing the coat and feeling very frumpy—much like a woman wearing a secondhand dyed coat!

Suddenly a woman on the opposite side of the wide sidewalk changed her direction and came over to me, and said with a smile, "I just have to tell you what a *beautiful* coat you have." She proceeded on her way before I could respond.

Afterward I wore that coat with pleasure through several winters, and have often thanked God for that stranger's thoughtfulness.

The Bible says, "Do not withhold good from those to whom it is due, when it is in your power to do it" (Proverbs 3:27). As I was thinking about this verse I realized this is a command from God, so when I fail to obey it, it is sin. Did you ever think it sin to *fail* to encourage or appreciate someone? Because God commands it, He is going to give the ability and many "nudgings" to speak up when we like something, and not to withhold that good word. At times we must ask God for an *awareness* to speak a word of appreciation. We take so much for granted, don't we (and then complain because our husbands seem to take us for granted!)? Have you thanked your husband lately for working long hours for you and the children? For coming home on time or calling you when he couldn't? For taking care of changing the oil in the car? For keeping the grass cut and shoveling the walks? Have you told him you are glad he chose you to marry, and that you appreciate his concern when you don't feel well?

And have you complimented him recently on those qualities you first fell in love with—his strength, his sense of humor, his brown eyes? Perhaps I have not hit one thing that is true about your husband. But think hard, my friend, and pray much concerning ways in which you can appreciate your husband and show him you adore him.

A number of years ago Jack had a skiing accident and ended up with his leg in a cast for six weeks. One evening as he was sitting on the hide-a-bed with his leg up after work, he looked at me and said, "Honey, you are too busy."

I glanced at him in surprise and then began a barrage of questions.

"Well, do you think I am neglecting you?" I asked.

"No," he responded.

"Do you think I am not giving enough attention to Lynn?"

"No," he said.

"Well, do you think I'm neglecting our home?"

"Perhaps, a little"—he softened that with a wry grin. "But that isn't what I mean."

Even with all my questions, he couldn't spell out exactly what he *did* mean, and it bothered me. I certainly didn't want to be too busy. But what was "too busy" and how was it affecting him? I had to say a frantic "Help, Lord."

God was faithful to reveal to me Jack's meaning. Jack, used to being very active, was suddenly restricted to the couch for all the evening hours and much of the weekends. On the other hand, I had curtailed none of my activities and had the extra care of waiting on him. While he was reading, studying and thinking, or watching television I would pull the ironing board into the living room to iron, or be running back and forth to the kitchen to wash, or working on a Bible study in the bedroom. I was too busy to relax with him and enjoy this extra time together which had been thrust upon us. And he felt it.

You may be sure I pared off all the low-priority items from my schedule and took the time to sit with him, to relax and talk. Jack is number two (my relationship with God being first) on my priority list, but I had forgotten this included relaxing with him.

One of the most effective ways to build into the life of your husband and let him know you appreciate him is by constantly assuring him that you are 100 percent *with him*. I remember vividly one time when I completely failed Jack in this.

It had been a period of utter frustration for me. We were in a Navigator home with four men living with us for training in Christian discipleship and to help lead our ministry. The work involved was staggering. But that wasn't my frustration, for I thrived on such responsibilities.

It was Jack. For several weeks he had been extremely distant, moody, and noncommunicative. Every time I tried to break through the wall of indifference (that was what it seemed like to me), the barrier seemed to get thicker. Even my withdrawal into a silence of my own (which is so unusual he almost always *has* to respond) went unnoticed. I began to feel like a part of the furniture, or at best a hired hand without pay, instead of a wife and companion. My attitude became worse and worse. But he seemingly didn't notice.

Finally I errupted! I walked into his study and let him have it—pow—right between the eyes in a verbal blast. I told him I was leaving for the day (Lynn had gone off to school), that I didn't know what time I would be back and I didn't know where I was going and didn't care, for I couldn't stand it any longer.

He did look at me then—*really* looked at me. I will never forget the wounded expression in his eyes as he said slowly, "Are you against me *too*?"

I had blasted the wall away all right, and all his bruised and infected wounds were revealed. He was undergoing severe criticism from some of those who were living in our home. He had been left stabbed and bleeding, and he had wanted to spare me from knowing his hurt. So he was trying to bear the pain all by himself, and in so doing had caused me to be "against" him too. I had completely misinterpreted the reason for his mood.

We wept together.

We agreed we would never again hide things from each other, and never try to endure injuries alone.

But what a lesson for this wife! At a time when Jack needed my confidence, my support, my help, I had let him down because I was not at that time 100 percent with him. It is a lesson I will never forget.

Our husbands need to know they have our support even when we don't agree with their decision. I am not talking about support of the decision, but of *them*—and there is quite a difference.

The president of our organization once asked a number of his men to answer a questionnaire containing this question: What do you most appreciate about your wife? I saw the compiled answers and immediately picked out the one my husband had written which said (bless him, he forgives so readily), "The thing I most appreciate about my wife is that she is 100 percent *with* me."

If we are to be "one" with our husbands, how can we *not* be totally supportive, affirming, and approving? They need our validation. And in a world that devalues, tears down, and corrodes, God grant that we should wave high the banner which reads, "Sweetheart, I support you."

Dear Father,
help me to build
into the life of my husband
by showing him I really am 'with him' . . .
by letting him see
that I appreciate and admire him.

*May he clearly hear
my languages of love.
Thank You.*

13 Enjoying Him

I${}$T IS THE TIME OF YEAR when the golden aspens color the mountains like bursts of sunshine. Yesterday Jack and I drove up near the historic Cripple Creek area to observe the spectacle. You have heard of a "riot of color"? Well this was more like a full-blown explosion. The cloudless, deep blue sky was a perfect backdrop for the shades of yellow splashing the mountains. At first it was an occasional burst among the evergreens, but as we drew nearer the high country the greens and yellows changed places, with only an occasional section of green splattered among the gold. I hope my mind recorded and stored the scenes in my treasure house of memories, because our man-made camera could not begin to capture the breathtaking beauty of the surroundings.

Driving back, I sighed with contentment. It was a perfect day, and there was no one in this world I would have rather shared it with than the man sitting beside me.

I turned to him then and asked, "Have we just naturally always enjoyed each other, or have there been some things we have consciously or unconsciously done that have helped us learn?" Jack grinned and answered in his usual, thoughtful way, "I'd have to think about that one."

In Scripture, Peter exhorts wives to win their husbands by their manner of life, behavior he describes as "chaste and reverent" (1 Peter 3:2, NEB). In the *Amplified New Testament*, which takes the original Greek and gives its expanded, various shades of meaning in English, this passage says, "That is, you are to feel for him all that reverence includes—to respect, defer to, revere him . . . to honor, esteem (appreciate, prize), and (in the human sense) adore him . . . to admire, praise, be devoted to, deeply love and enjoy (your husband)."

Recently a friend told me, "I never talk to my husband about any of my interests, because he is only concerned with his work and he feels threatened by any of my pastimes"—a sad state of affairs indeed.

While sharing the interests of one's partner should definitely be a two-way street, I am not writing to husbands, but to wives. So let me ask you, do you share your husband's interests?

Lois Wyse expresses it this way:

> *"Someone asked me*
>   *to name the time*
> *Our friendship stopped*
>   *and love began.*
> *Oh, my darling,*
>   *that's the secret.*
> *Our friendship*
>   *never stopped."*[1]

A part of creating a lasting friendship includes genuine interest in those things that excite our husbands.

Linda Dillow writes, "I have a dear friend whose husband is an avid fisherman. When they were newly married, he suggested they go fishing. Because she had heard that the family that plays together, stays together, she went. She recounted that the first time she put a minnow on a fishing hook, she was sure she would vomit. As with most things, it got easier, until soon she could do it without closing her eyes!

"Now, many years and four children later, she is thankful she became interested in her husband's interests. She recently said, 'Linda, do you know the best time Bruce and I had last year? It was at 6:00 A.M. cleaning fish by the lake. The children were asleep, and we talked of deep and wonderful things we rarely talk about as we cleaned the fish. I thanked God that morning that I had been willing to put that first minnow on the hook.'"[2]

This summer a man who attended one of our weekend marriage seminars said to Jack and me, "There is one thing you *must* add to what you say to couples."

"What is that?" we inquired.

He responded, "You must tell them every couple should have a motorcycle!"

We laughed, but he stopped us. "No, I'm serious. I'm not talking about a literal motorcycle. I'm talking about something that they really enjoy doing together."

Then he related how, as a middle-aged couple, he and his wife realized they didn't have a lot of things in common which they really enjoyed doing together for recreation. They discussed it and he reached far back into his pent-up dreams and bought a fully equipped motorcycle (complete with a stereo tape deck!). His wife, a short woman who can't even reach the ground when she sits on the back of the cycle, loves to eat out. So they devised a plan. He didn't care where they headed as long as they were cruising the roads together on his beloved motorcycle. And she plotted their trips to some interesting and unusual restaurants in California. She would carry a better outfit in the little "trunk" on the cycle to change into later, or wear it under her motorcycle coveralls, and away they would go. He said it has been a wonderful way of bringing them closer together. They have both enjoyed their times because of their motorcycle. Then he repeated again, "You must tell couples that they each should have a 'motorcycle'—something they really enjoy together."

As I looked back over the years, I realized this was something Jack and I have worked on without being conscious of it. I was thoroughly turned off in college by young women who pretended to be interested in football and sports only to snare a fellow they were attracted to. Early, I asked God for a *real* interest. I must admit sometimes my mind was boggled from listening to football plays over a coke at the Student Union, but it helped me become really interested in football. Today, though I am not excited about all the pro teams (fortunately neither is Jack), I get genuinely absorbed when we occasionally go to a college game, or when I know a player on the team, or when the Denver Broncos reach the Super Bowl!

On the other hand, Jack takes an interest in my involvement in crafts. He doesn't do them, he just comments encouragingly when I do. It isn't always the involvement together that is important. It is the interest one takes in what the other is involved in that is imperative.

However, involvement together in at least one or two things is important as a means of building friendship. If your husband isn't willing to search for something you both enjoy, then I believe God will give you the ability to adapt to his interest.

As a result of a "marital intimacy" test some time

ago, Jack and I discovered that we rated lowest on "recreational intimacy." He has always been athletic and that is not one of my strong suits (the understatement of the year!).

As we talked about it we decided to take up tennis together, which I have learned to love. I also determined that after 25 years of being a spectator I would take up golf. Jack loves to play golf and our vacations usually include someplace where there is a beautiful course. While I have always enjoyed driving the cart for him, it isn't always possible on crowded courses, so three years ago I decided to try to learn to play. I have had to pray for two things: a genuine liking for it (I knew I'd never really pursue it if I didn't like it), and enough ability not to feel like an utter fool. God has given me the first; the second I'm still praying for! It may have me licked but even if I sell my clubs, having taken some lessons and playing for three summers has given me a much greater appreciation of Jack's skill, and I will have even more fun driving his cart while on vacation.

There is another ingredient to enjoyment. Some husbands and wives don't enjoy each other because of one spouse's irritating habit—some glaring fault in one's behavior that prevents true enjoyment of the other's company. I have heard such comments as: "I don't enjoy going out to eat because my husband's manners are so crude" . . . "My wife is so disconnected in her speech I can't converse with her" . . . "In all our years together, my wife has never complimented me" . . . "I feel like he is mad at me much of the time" . . . "He completely withdraws and won't talk when we are alone" . . . "She has let herself go and doesn't try to be attractive, and I'm ashamed to take her out."

So lack of enjoyment sometimes is due to simply not

liking some aspect of behavior in the other person. What can be done about this?

We looked earlier at Proverbs 27:17: "Iron sharpens iron, so one man sharpens another." We may sometimes forget that this is one of the purposes of marriage. When iron is sharpening iron, sparks fly! Only in the pain of the flying sparks is it possible to be sharpened.

Some of you are probably going to misunderstand what I am about to say. We read so much about accepting our mates just as they are, and how it is our job to make them happy and God's job to make them good. Both of these statements are completely true.

However, the other side of the coin is that God brought us together to learn from one another, to sharpen each other, to become better people because of each other, and to adjust to each other. Granted, to deal with negatives about the other requires maturity on the part of both. It requires both people working at a relationship and being willing to change. Some women may be saying, "But my husband isn't willing to listen or to change." There is only one thing you can do in this case, but it is enough. That is to pray for him. I mean *really* pray for him. Put all those things you'd like to confront him with on a prayer list, and pray for him every day. Most of all, pray that you will love and accept him and that God will give you the ability to adjust to him and to overlook (and even *love*) those very things that are irritating you now. Then pray that he will be open to talk about some of the other things. But most of all pray that you will be willing to change behavior that is irritating to him, even though he is unwilling to change behavior that is ugly to you.

We can't change our husbands. Only God can. Conversely, they can't change us. But God can, and He can make us willing to listen to our husbands, to be open to them, and to help us adjust in ways that will make us more enjoyable to be with. I really believe that when we become more fun to be with, our husbands will, for the most part, agree to change for us too.

I used to wear bobby pins in my hair until I discovered it was irritating to Jack to have them poke his cheek when I put my head on his shoulder. So I changed my hairstyle. It was a small thing.

But my tendency to "boss" and take over in situations that are not my responsibility at all is part of my independent Dutch background. I have had to pray, struggle, and surrender time and time again, because there are still traces of that tendency lying around ready to surface at precisely the wrong time. But God and I are working at it, because Jack doesn't like it, and I don't like it either!

In a thousand little ways we have adjusted, discarding annoying habits and praying to accept traits that could not be changed. We have grown to enjoy one another in a deeper way each year as we have adapted to each other.

So what do you do if your husband's manners are so crude you don't enjoy dining out with him? Well, if he is open to suggestion, take a class in etiquette together or read a bit of Emily Post as a family (maybe your children need it too!), and discuss each principle that is important to you. If your manner of speaking irritates your husband, read a book on communication and get a friend to help you say what is on your mind in a more direct way. The name of the game is *change*. And it is a game we can win as we claim the promise of Philippians 4:13: "I can do all things through Him who strengthens me."

When was the last time your husband or someone else made a suggestion to you, and you said (or thought), "But that's just the way I am"?

When was the last time *God* showed you something

you should alter? If He doesn't do it frequently, you have stopped listening!

What is on your prayer list concerning changes that need to take place in your life and personality, your husband's life and personality, and your children's lives? What is on your prayer list concerning interests you as a couple can share? Are you praying that you will have more fun together? That you will be better friends? That you will enjoy one another increasingly?

God indeed is magnificent. He wants to delight you. He *delights* to delight you. But He waits to be asked, for He will not force anything on us.

> *Dear Lord,*
> *Help us as a couple*
> *to learn to be best friends . . .*
> *to delight in and enjoy one another*
> *in ever-increasing ways and depths.*
> *Thank You.*

"Two are better than one because they have a good return for heir labor. For if either of them falls, the one will lift up his companion. But woe to the one who falls when there is not another to lift him up" (Ecclesiastes 4:9-10).

> *Lord,*
> *What a beautiful picture*
> *of marriage!*
> *Not two halves of a couple,*
> *but two people*
> *being and doing*
> *more together*
> *than they could have been*

or done
  alone.
Not just double effectiveness,
  but multiplied!
An integral part
  of marriage
  is being all I was meant to be
    as a person . . .
    and even more!
Thank You for giving me a
  partner who makes me
  know that this is
    TRUE!
      Amen

1. "Non-Stop" by Lois Wyse, *Love Poems for the Very Married* (© 1967 by Lois Wyse), page 41. Reprinted by permission of Harper and Row, Publishers, Inc.
2. Linda Dillow, *Creative Counterpart*, page 97.

PART THREE
Wisdom for a Mother

14 Building by Example

"CAROLE, I am not going to tell you not to smoke." Mother's brown eyes were serious as I looked up in surprise at her startling remark. A few of my girlfriends had begun to experiment with smoking "behind the barn," and Mother and I were discussing it. I knew my parents disapproved of smoking so I was quite shocked by her initial statement.

She continued, "I cannot be either your judge or your keeper as you are growing up, so I am not going to tell you that you must not smoke." She paused and then said, "But I am going to ask you to promise me that you will smoke your first cigarette *in front of me*."

In our household, a promise was not given lightly. It might as well be a sacred oath sworn on the Bible. To my knowledge my parents never broke a promise to me. If they weren't sure about something, they wouldn't promise. We were expected to act just as honorably.

Therefore I took Mother's request seriously. And I thought it was a reasonable request. In fact it was ingenious! When my friends asked me to smoke I could say,

"Well, my mom says she won't object at all! So I can do it if I want to. But I promised to smoke my first one in her presence so you'll have to wait awhile."

A wise woman, my mother. I didn't know it when I promised that day, but she had just taken all the wicked fun out of sneaking off somewhere to smoke with friends. To this day, I have never had a cigarette in my lips—because who in their right mind would smoke their first in front of a mother whom they loved and respected, and whom they knew would be heartbroken to watch them?

Mother and Dad built many things into the lives of their three children, concepts that we have passed on to our children and which I trust will be continued in the lives of their sons and daughters.

"Train up a child in the way he should go, even when he is old he will not depart from it" (Proverbs 22:6) is a verse that is oft-quoted to parents. It is given as an admonition to train their children. Parents frequently claim this promise for their sons and daughters.

But at least one thing must be realized. The old statement rings true that "telling is not teaching; listening is not learning; and teaching is not training." This verse says to *train* a child. Perhaps we need to ask ourselves if we are telling, teaching, or actually training our children in Christ. We should be doing all three. Often parents do only the first.

Jack and I have had the opportunity to work with many young people who have been raised in Christian homes and who attended Christian schools. In many cases we have observed a lack of spiritual reality in their lives. The children know all the right words, but their lives have not been affected.

As I look back on my own home it isn't the "devotional times" that were planned which stand out. In fact, I remember these as being something that had little meaning at the time. It was seeing Mother come from her room with tears on her cheeks after communing intimately with God. It was observing Dad graciously welcome his widowed mother-in-law into our home to live with us for 17 years—years of increasing senility and depression for her. It was witnessing his attitude of kindness, patience, fairness, and love. It was seeing Mother give of herself and her time to help people in need. It was recognizing love in action, and glimpsing the flow of God's Spirit in the daily routine of our lives.

It dawned on me then that training is grasped by example.

Marian was just putting the meringue on a dessert for a dinner party of 24 and placing it in the oven to brown, when she looked out the window and saw her little boy, Randy, topple over the swing set he was playing on. She ran out to see if he was hurt. Finding him to be in one piece, she paused to thank the Lord with Randy for God's protection. By the time she came into the house, smoke was pouring from the oven. The meringue was burned black and hard. Instead of exploding, she calmly scraped the burned meringue off the dessert, took some whipping cream from the freezer and prepared the dessert once again.

As I saw her reaction, several things came to mind. I realized it was her natural reaction to pause and thank God with her child rather than have her mind on the importance of her company's dessert. I knew this attitude came only from having a deep relationship with God. I understood also that training takes place in the context of our lives. If Randy had seen his mother upset instead of praising God with him, she would not be able to tell him to "be anxious for nothing" (Philippians 4:6) without contradicting the example of her actions. If I had observed anger and frustration during that incident, I would not have been so challenged to go deep with God—so deep that my own reactions could reflect Him.

God chose to give Jack and me only one precious child. Because of this, we rarely talk about raising children even though Lynn has become a committed servant of God. We really don't have any way to discern if she turned out well in spite of us or because of us. We do know it was all from God's grace.

Many good books have been written by people far more experienced and qualified to speak about raising children than I am. But I feel compelled to share a few principles which were profitable for us in building into the life of our child. The first principle is that we *build by example*. We cannot expect children to do what we are not doing, and to be what we are not being. But by letting God work deeply in our lives, by dwelling daily in His Word, by practicing the presence of God moment by moment in prayer, we will be "becomers"—being conformed to the image of Christ, and showing our children the example of the reality of God. This can be our prayer:

Oh, Lord. I fall so short of being a reflection of You. Teach me, first of all what it means to love You with all my heart, my strength, my mind. And then show me how to live before my children in such a way that You will be seen.
Thank You.

15 Building by Teaching

"**M**OTHER!" Lynn exclaimed plaintively. "I think you have given me such a hang-up that I'll never enjoy kissing! I think I will feel so guilty that I'll never like it!"

Inside, I couldn't help but grin as I thought, *O sweetheart, that will never be a problem for you!*

But Lynn was sixteen, auburn-haired and vivacious, wanting to experience life all at once and *right then*. The thoughts running through my mind at that moment would not have been a wise retort.

As Lynn grew up, we had spent hours discussing standards of purity, dating, kissing, and petting. Now she was feeling all alone and frustrated because her standards were not shared even by other Christian girls she knew. When the leaders of a Christian high school group she had joined began talking about purity, they didn't start with kissing. They began their discussions with petting.

I am convinced that the phrase "too little, too late" describes most training in the area of physical involvement through the dating years. Some parents wait until dating age and as the child is dressing for that first date, they say,

"Now be careful." Well, this is an exaggeration for most, I'm sure. But because of the pressures of our world system and the bombardment of low standards on television and from their peers, we need to start early—even before they start to talk—and *train* our children in godliness.

Our first step may need to be an examination of God's Word to find out what His standard is. Most of our generation has been brainwashed, squeezed into the world's mold in our thinking to such a degree that we need to be renewed with God's perspective before we can adequately think about training our children. Stephen Olford's book *The Sanctity of Sex* is a good starting place. But there is no substitute for an in-depth study of God's Word for oneself. In many areas, we Christians have been carried along with the flood of the world's thinking, and deposited on the sands a few miles farther down the stream of liberalism. Every few months, we are pushed a few feet more. Some of us may tug at the bottom for balance; but battered by the rocks of shaky standards and the tidewater of the world, most of us keep getting shoved along. We need to be lodged against the Rock that won't allow us to be moved. We must examine our beliefs by the Word of God and not budge another inch (we may even need to back up a few feet!). We need to ask God to cleanse our hearts from preconceived ideas and the taint of the world's outlook, and we must come up with our own Rock-bound convictions that cannot be swayed.

When Lynn was in the fifth grade she came home once all excited about a record party she had been invited to—a boy-girl party. No, she didn't know if the parents were going to be there. No, she didn't know exactly what one did at a record party. But she was eager to go.

I took a deep breath, prayed for wisdom, and said, "Honey, we can't let you go this time."

Her face fell and she wailed, "But Mother, *why not*?"

It was a valid question. Our rule-of-the-house was to never say no unless we had to—but when we had to, to stick with it, and explain as best we could all of our reasoning behind the decision.

"Honey, if you start going to boy-girl parties at age 10, you will be ready to date singly at age 11 or 12, and be going steady at 13 or 14. We have talked about the dangers of going steady. You have lots of time to date and to go to parties. This is just too soon. It would be rushing things and there would be situations you just aren't old enough to handle."

We probably spent another two hours talking about this before she really saw things in perspective. And I think she was secretly relieved that she could reply "My folks won't let me" to that invitation.

Having an only child has some advantages. It gives a parent literally hundreds of hours alone with that child. Lynn and I had discussed often and at great length the teenage dating years in relation to marriage—the four to eight years of dating as they relate to the rest of your life. So often (and quite naturally), young people cannot think beyond *this* moment, *this* day, *this* date. Because of that, they get themselves into a great deal of trouble. They need to see dating and the purposes of dating at various stages of growing up in light of the rest of their lives. And that doesn't happen in one conversation. My mother used to tell me that if God had someone for me to marry, in God's eyes I was already engaged. What a help this was in taking a long-range view and in keeping myself for that person.

The purpose for dating in high school is at least threefold. First, for fun. This is a legitimate reason. We do a lot of things for fun and recreation and this can be one of them. Second, to learn to better relate to the opposite sex, to understand them, and to be friends. And third, to have some basis of comparison when a life partner is chosen later on.

You may think of other purposes also, but one thing is needful: These purposes should line up with one's whole life and value system.

Now what part does physical involvement have to do with any of these purposes for dating? The answer would have to be *absolutely none*. In fact, physical involvement takes away from really getting to know each other as a person. It can create needless heartache, headache, and frustration, besides being a wrong basis of comparison later on. And it can wreck a life!

Today most Christian parents don't begin with this kind of teaching. They begin with why their sons and daughters shouldn't pet or have intercourse outside of marriage. Lynn and I had begun with the value of a kiss and decided that it was a very special something to be saved for someone valued highly in her life. "Someone valued" had not entered the picture by age sixteen. Hence her wail about my giving her "hang-ups." She has a good laugh about this herself now.

The world tells us:

(1) Our problems are due to feelings of guilt because of past Puritan ethics. The reasoning is that our ancestors thought sex was wrong. They had conservative beliefs which have caused many problems. The world's solution to this is that sex is not wrong anytime or anyplace. The more sex we have the more our guilt feelings and difficulties will diminish.

(2) When you love someone, it is wrong and selfish to leave them frustrated by not giving them all you have.

(3) Sex is healthy and right anytime. It is only our attitude that is wrong.

(4) There is no real authority or standard anyway. Everything is relative. Nothing is really wrong.

(5) Sex is like any other bodily function and we shouldn't give it so much meaning. Why should it hurt more to break up with a man you have slept with, than with one you haven't? If we didn't give sex so much importance no one would get hurt.

What a faulty, ugly bill of goods we are urged to buy! To allow the world's philosophies to become entrenched in our thinking is to destroy the depth of beauty God intended when He created sex for marriage.

In *The Stork Is Dead*, Charlie Shedd puts it like this:

"Did you ever raise peanuts? I did. Nothing so great about that because we lived in the country. Most country boys raise something. But this was new to me, and I don't recommend it for nine-year-olds.

"The problem is that peanuts grow underground. You hoe and water and wait. You watch the tops grow. But are there any peanuts? What if there aren't any peanuts?

"So I did the worst thing you can imagine. One day when my folks weren't home, I pulled up my peanuts to see. Not bad! Some half-grown, nice shape, very promising. Of course, I packed the earth around them again and waited now with confidence.

"But you know what happened. You should only dig peanuts once. When you do it more often, you shatter their nervous system. They turn out funny. They get long and flat or nubby and wide. They twist and take on the oddest shapes. Some of them rot and they die. To say the least, the whole thing was awful.

"Life is like my peanut crop in so many places. Many a teenager has learned the hard way that some things can't be hurried.

"So this is a good thing to remember:

"YOU MIGHT TEAR UP SOMETHING THAT
NEEDS MORE TIME IF YOU GET STARTED WITH
SEX TOO SOON!"[1]

The journey through the growing up years is very
treacherous indeed! Our children need all the help we can
give them.

Supposing Lynn had to go on a very dangerous,
frightening journey over difficult terrain. Imagine I had
been over this territory many times before and knew that if
she took an incorrect fork in the trail, she would fall off a
cliff. A wrong road at another place would head her into a
dangerous swamp. A bridge was out along one stretch, and
many other dangers threatened her journey. But I knew
that a good, safe road went right through to her destina-
tion.

What kind of a mother would I be if I kissed her goodbye as she began her trip and said, "Well, good luck. Hope
you make it safely." That would be terrible! The least a
loving mother would do would be to draw her a detailed
map with many guidelines. And the best thing would be to
say, "Hey, why don't I go along with you and guide you?"

God has done exactly that! Psalm 119:19 says, "I am
but a pilgrim here on earth: how I need a map—and your
commands are my chart and guide" (LB).

Isn't that wonderful? The Bible is our map—our chart
and guide.

But God doesn't stop there. He has promised to go
with us, never to forsake us—our guide and friend all the
way. All we need to do is to *pay attention* to Him. He will
never force us against our wills to go in the direction He
tells us.

Parents, we need to let God teach *us* first of all about

what purity and godliness mean. Then we need to communicate, and communicate, and communicate with our children on this subject. Our children have more pressures than we can imagine *against* what God says is right. We need great wisdom and lots of time to counteract this teaching, and even more wisdom and time to teach what is positive and true.

Otherwise, our children may shipwreck their lives.

Remember the story of Jacob and Esau? Esau was the older brother and had the right to a greater inheritance. But one night he came in from hunting, very hungry, and his brother, Jacob, was cooking up a pot of soup. When Esau asked Jacob for some soup, Jacob said, "Sure, if you will give me the right to your greater inheritance." And Esau, without a second thought, agreed to this bargain. He sold his birthright for a bowl of soup! He gave away his inheritance to fulfill a momentary pang of hunger!

This is what we do if we dabble in the momentary pleasure of the here and now at the expense of the rest of our lives! We are taken in by the philosophy of songs like "To Wait for Love Is Just to Waste Your Life Away."

God forbid that we allow our minds to become so saturated with this kind of poisonous thinking that we are blind to its intent. May we ask God for a fresh cleansing of His Spirit through the Word of God and a clarity of conviction so we may build into our children's lives.

---

1. Charlie Shedd, *The Stork Is Dead* (Waco, Texas: Word Books, 1968), page 18. © 1968 by Charlie Shedd and the Abundance Foundation. Used by permission of Word Books.

16 Courageous Training

I DUBBED HIM "JOE COURAGE." He was a tiny brown squirrel with a thin, scraggly tail, bright, ever-vigilant eyes, and jerky movements. Each afternoon we would hear a scratching on the large balcony of the condominium where we were vacationing, and there, outside the glass patio door, would be Joe Courage looking at us intently. If no peanuts were forthcoming, he'd scurry up one side of the wooden door frame and around the top, peering upside down every few seconds into our living room. Then he would scamper down the other side of the frame, flicking his tail reprovingly. His nervous movements displayed a fear of humans, but his courageous heart made him brave the terror. In our week's stay Joe Courage became a friend.

I gave him that name because God was impressing me that week about courage. I needed to be impressed! The previous week I had faced some difficult and trying problems. I had lost the battle and gone down in flaming discouragement.

Courage is defined as "the attitude of facing and dealing with anything recognized as dangerous, difficult, or painful, instead of withdrawing from it . . . being fearless or brave."[1] Lorne Sanny, president of The Navigators, suggests that courage is simply the "mental discipline to endure."

These days people, especially parents, need a great deal of courage. Writing on the need for training our children about dating, sex, and marriage, Howard and Jeanne Hendricks speak of "an unashamedly agressive thrust" which parents need.[2]

Paul told Timothy to train himself in godliness (1 Timothy 4:7). This is our task, and we have the responsibility to train our children in godliness as well. And this takes courage.

God's plan is that we should be holy and pure. If you have invited Jesus Christ into your life, He has already made you righteous. Scripture says, "Blessed be the God and Father of our Lord Jesus Christ, who has blessed us with every spiritual blessing in the heavenly places in Christ, just as He chose us in Him before the foundation of the world, that we should be *holy* and *blameless* before Him" (Ephesians 1:3-4). This is what we may call positional righteousness.

But His plan also includes *actual* purity. God is in the business of conforming us to the image of His Son, perfecting us, and making our lives holy and honoring to Him so that we will have a pure, peaceable, and joyous existence.

God's standards are far different from the world's. He has given us His standards, not to deny us anything that would make us happy, but for our lifelong good. This is the concept we must get across to our children. God wants the best for *all* our lives. He has the long-range view. And He says, "Avoid sexual looseness like the plague!

Every other sin that a man commits is done outside his own body, but this is an offense against his own body. Have you forgotten that your body is the temple of the Holy Spirit, who lives in you and is God's gift to you, and that you are not the owner of your own body? You have been bought, and at a price! Therefore bring glory to God in your body" (1 Corinthians 6:18-20, PH).

Purity of life means many things. It means purity of thought, intent, and deed. But in Scripture one very prominent meaning is sexual purity. Intercourse, petting, and loose conduct apart from marriage is spelled out in the Bible as very wrong.

God wants the best for us. He wants us to be truly free, happy, and spiritually healthy. "God's plan is to make you holy, and that means a clean cut with sexual immorality. Every one of you should learn to control his body, keeping it pure and treating it with respect, and never allowing it to fall victim to lust, as do pagans with no knowledge of God. You cannot break this rule without cheating and exploiting your fellow-men. Indeed God will punish all who do offend in this matter, as we have plainly told you and warned you. The calling of God is not to impurity but to the most thorough purity, and anyone who makes light of the matter is not making light of a man's ruling but of God's command. It is not for nothing that the Spirit God gives us is called the *Holy* Spirit" (1 Thessalonians 4:3-8, PH).

I have talked to any number of wives who, for one reason or another, have had an affair before marriage, or hadn't waited until marriage to be with the one they eventually did marry. The tragic stories vary but have one central thread—"I wish I hadn't done it." Many times there seems to be something preventing a young wife from fully and completely responding to her husband within marriage. She fights a long battle with comparison, guilt, and wrong perspective, and it may take years to find a way to win this war.

Our children must have convictions, firm and strong, *before* they get into situations that are tempting.

> "In the life of the average teenager there will be some intense moments. When they come, the only help available may be your predetermined policy. What you are may *show up* in the crisis. But it is almost sure to have been *made up* long before you got there."[3]

The training in godliness starts the moment a child is born. If we wait until a child is nearly a teenager, we have waited too long. We must teach our children early the beauty of sex within marriage—that sex is total commitment and communion, a knowledge of one another in body, soul, and spirit. Sex can be all this in marriage, the context for which God created it.

Proverbs 5 makes a valuable study for a parent and child to do together. In this chapter it is clear that the end of adultery for a woman is bitterness, death, and instability (Proverbs 5:4-6). For a man it means less vigor, wasted years, disease, and sometimes utter ruin (Proverbs 5:7-14).

This chapter reveals the vivid contrast of beautiful married love with a cheap affair. God's desire is for sex in marriage to be like a deep well fed by a fresh, bubbling fountain that will quench our thirst, never taste stale or impure, and give us exhilarating joy. This produces a knowledge of each other that cannot be gained in any other way: a lasting and total involvement. But the fountain becomes clogged and the well becomes shallow and polluted when we dissipate the water by splashing it about in little puddles of casual relationships. And anything outside of marriage is a casual relationship in the eyes of God!

Sometimes we think of God as not wanting us to have any fun! The reverse is true. God wants us to have the most wonderful kinds of fun, and joy, and exhilaration! But this is only possible when we follow His advice.

We must teach our children that they are being cheated if they think they can go "all the way" apart from marriage. Charlie Shedd puts it this way:

"Over and over and over I hear it. My letters are loaded with 'All the Way!' . . . 'He says we'll be married some day so why not go all the way?' . . . 'In our school they call you a freak if you don't go all the way!' . . . 'Can you tell me why if we love each other we shouldn't go all the way?'

"Yes, I can tell you! I can tell you that what you are talking about actually isn't even halfway. It isn't a fourth, or an eighth, or a thirty-second. It's not even one small percentage of what you want. What you call 'all the way' sex is really only 'semi-sex' and very second-rate.

"At its best sex is a total involvement. It is the total involvement of your whole emotional makeup with the whole emotional makeup of one other person.

"There is a major fallacy abroad that sex is simply the act of intercourse. But it is so much more than that. In a very real sense sex is not just something you do. When it is right, it is something that you and the person you love are becoming together. This has its roots way down at the center of the universe permanently and forever. The truth is that 'All the Way' sex at its greatest isn't free. Sex like it ought to be is only for those who will pay the price of total commitment."[4]

We must ask God for the ability to train our children to understand His divine purpose for intercourse with all its beauty, sacredness, and delight. Our goal is to train children to have the mind of Christ, and to see God's plan for life from His perspective and not our own limited view. We must communicate God's precious plan for sex within marriage and the disastrous consequence of not heeding His plan. To do this will take courage, time and wisdom. "With God all things are possible" (Matthew 19:26).

---

1. With permission. From *Webster's New World Dictionary*, Second College Edition, © 1978 by William Collins and World Publishing Co., Inc., page 338.
2. Howard G. and Jeanne Hendricks, "Preparing Young People for Christian Marriage," in *Ventures in Family Living*, edited by Roy B. Zuck and Gene A. Getz (Chicago: Moody Press, 1971), page 54.
3. Charlie Shedd, *The Stork Is Dead*, page 28.
4. Shedd, *The Stork Is Dead*, pages 20-21.

17 Purity and Godliness

TWO WOMEN HAD PRECEDED ME out of the home in which we had just been meeting. Observing us outside was a three-year-old girl sitting astride her tricycle, her blond hair tied in two neat ponytails. She watched each one of us intently as we left the house and walked toward our cars. As I came opposite her, she shook her head in frustration and with an offended air said, "Three moms and no *kids*?"

Well, this mom only had one "kid" and she is a girl, so of necessity I am writing this chapter on purity from the perspective of teaching girls. The translation to boys will have to be yours, I'm afraid.

Some specific areas of purity need our attention before we can truly instruct our children in godliness. It would be impossible to speak to all areas, so my goal is to give food for thought and prayer in order to stimulate thorough, individual study on the subject. Each of our circumstances is different and I can't place my convictions on you, nor would I want to. My plea is only that you do some thinking and praying for yourselves.

In the seventh chapter of Proverbs, a woman is described who is up to no good. Looking at her characteristics may give us guidelines to aspects of behavior which women need to avoid:

This woman is dressed as a harlot (verse 10). She was deliberately out to entice a man by being "cunning of heart." She was enticing in her words, forward in her conduct, flattering in her manner, and bold in her behavior—not a pretty picture, and perhaps not one we initially identify with. But let's take a closer look.

The first thing mentioned about this woman is the way she dressed.

A friend of Lynn's, every inch a man, wrote to her about this very thing and said, "You see, originally, had Adam and Eve not botched it, we'd have no problem. But as it is now, people need to be careful of how physical they become. A corny word called modesty is in line here. Now I'm no Victorian, but the purpose of a bikini is the sexually revealing aspect of it—specifically to excite men. How can a Christian woman wear one?"

One summer Lynn and her husband Tim had the opportunity to ask a group of single fellows of college age some significant questions concerning areas which caused them problems in their thoughts. The answers were helpful. In the area of dress, the question was asked, "What women's clothing presents temptation or is distracting?" All of the men said that low necklines, short shorts, tight garments, and see-through blouses were a problem. Others indicated that halters, midriffs, and a bra that shows also bothered them.

Jesus said, "It is inevitable that stumbling blocks come; but woe to that man through whom the stumbling block comes!" (Matthew 18:7). Now I am for dressing as beautifully as I can afford. God has made me a "princess"—a child of the King. And as a princess, I need to dress as tastefully and attractively as I can.

But another consideration is to be careful not to be a temptation for a fellow believer lest I cause problems in his thought life.

An important concern here, it seems to me, is to not wear anything that brings immediate attention to *me*. I want Christ to show through. Our objective is not to "appear in all our glory" but to disappear for His glory—to be mirrors reflecting Christ. For instance, if I don't wear any makeup among a group of models I will be known only as "that woman who doesn't wear makeup," and the attention is focused on the "reflector" rather than on Christ. On the other hand, if I wear ostentatious jewelry among individuals who wear little or none, they will focus on my jewelry instead of on Christ—the Jewel in my life.

If my dress brings attention to any specific part of my anatomy . . . especially to parts that would bring tempting thoughts to a man's mind, I am not really glorifying Christ because I have hindered that person from seeing Christ in me.

Most women are completely and totally unaware of how men think. Because it wouldn't bother *them* to see a woman wearing a T-shirt saying "It's what's inside that counts" on it, they blithely think it shouldn't bother a man. Mothers, we need to find out from our husbands just what a man's thinking is. Then we need to train our daughters to be aware of how easily some men are stimulated to think thoughts they really don't want to think. Now, granted, we don't want to make a daughter self-conscious about herself and think that every man is mentally undressing her, but we do need to impart some principles which will help her choose her wardrobe for the rest of her life.

The next thing Proverbs 7 talks about is a woman's manner, or how she acts. The men responding to Tim and Lynn's questionnaire had some interesting things to say about this too.

To the question "What other things (besides dress) are distracting to you?" their answers included flirting with the eyes, not sitting properly, lying down, and making leading comments. One Christian leader told some teenage girls when mini-styles were in vogue, "Don't think a fellow feels it is an accident when he sees the edge of your panties. He thinks you are showing it on purpose and it becomes a problem to him."

The men interviewed had some positive things to say as well. When asked, "What do you appreciate about Christian women?" they were found to like women who didn't strive for attention and who found their security in God. They appreciated women who did not flirt, who were modest in their dress, and who were sensitive to the feelings of men. They respected a woman of worth, a woman whose beauty was in her character.

Godliness is not a list of do's and don'ts. The specific things mentioned in this chapter are only to give concrete ideas in a few areas. We need to train our children in heart attitudes, in obedience to God, and in love for others. We need to show them the reason behind being careful how we dress. The truth of 1 Corinthians 8:12 must be planted in their hearts: "By sinning against the brethren and wounding their conscience when it is weak, you sin against Christ." The principle expressed in 1 Peter 3:3-4 must become their conviction: "Let not your adornment be external only—braiding the hair, and wearing gold jewelry, and putting on dresses; but let it be the hidden person of the heart, with the imperishable quality of a gentle and quiet spirit, which is precious in the sight of God."

God looks on the heart. He examines our motives, our intents, our attitudes, our character. But to everyone but God, it is only what we *do* that tells them who we are. Understanding this is essential to being an ambassador for our Lord.

Let this be your prayer:

"Father, I really need wisdom in this area. I don't want to put my children in a box, to become legalistic with do's and don'ts. Help me to train them in godliness, to teach them the principles behind the rules. Help me also put cement in the framework of those principles so they may walk firmly.

Thank You."

18 The Most Important Inheritance

A RECENT MAGAZINE article[1] tells of Amy, a straight-A student who hanged herself after receiving her first B at age 15. She left this note:

> "Mom and Dad have never said anything to me about having to get good grades. In fact, we rarely talk about it. But I know they do not want nor could they tolerate a failure. And if I fail in what I do, I fail in what I am. Goodbye."

A recent rash of such articles on teenage suicide made a deep impression on me. The one which told about Amy also said that children commit suicide because they are taught that happiness is found in things, in what you do, in conforming, or in being free of problems—all of which are incorrect concepts to teach our children.

In another article, I read this:

> "Parents strive to give their children happiness, not by a search for what is fulfilling, but by an avoidance of what

presents difficulties. They eliminate boredom by crowding a year-round schedule with activities; they eliminate failure by rationalizing its causes and preventing accountability; they eliminate conflict by avoiding confrontations; they eliminate effort by doing things for their children. Children grow up then, not only self-indulgent, but lacking in confidence. Their overprotective parents have instilled in them a feeling of 'I can't cope.' Therefore, when trouble arises, they are ill prepared to face it. Frequently, suicide turns up as a possible answer."[2]

We are told much about giving our children wrong values and the results of doing so. We are even told what to do: We are to "communicate," demonstrate love, be accepting, and teach correct values. Sometimes we are also given good advice as to how to communicate or to demonstrate love. But rarely are we told how to acquire the ability and power to communicate when it requires great effort. It is difficult to show love when we are completely exhausted, and it is almost impossible to show love when we feel hated. If we feel rejected ourselves it is hard to truly accept others, or to teach the values that will hold a child's life together. Few answers are provided to ensure the raising of morally and emotionally healthy children in an immoral and unhealthy world.

It is a frightening matter to bring a child into the world and assume full responsibility for that precious life. For us, it would have been *too* fearful if we hadn't had some deep assurance that we didn't have to do it alone. It was too awesome a task to "hope for the best"—to base our guidance of this intricate soul on the conflicting views of men. We needed a more dependable method. Our conviction was, and is, that the only sure place to turn is to God as He speaks through His Word.

Before Jack and I had a child, we spent much time asking God not to allow us to have a baby unless that child would grow up to love and honor Him. Because of His foreknowledge, perhaps that is the reason God chose to give us only one. But Lynn has grown up to love and serve God, as does Tim, her husband. We prayed a great deal for Tim even before we knew him! We had specific requests for whoever God chose as a husband for Lynn if she was to marry, and our first request was that he would love God with his whole heart and desire to serve Him. As we prayed specifically, God answered in the same manner. Tim is all we prayed for, with a number of bonuses thrown in. And now another generation is beginning.

When Lynn was three months pregnant, she called one day all bubbly and happy. She said, "Mom, I just listened to the baby's heartbeat!" and we rejoiced together over the fully formed three-and-a-half-inch person inside her that modern technology had allowed her to hear at three months. We were thrilled at the thought of being grandparents! We wondered at times who was the most excited at the prospect: the parents, the great-grandparents (this was their first great-grandchild), or us. It was a close contest.

I loved the thought of being a grandmother! But it was a sobering thought as, looking at our world's crumbling morals and permissive society, one contemplated the responsibility of parents today. So I began to pray for my grandchild while he was still in Lynn's womb. Lynn and Tim will need God's wisdom and grace to teach the reality of His truth to their children—truths such as "May the God of peace Himself make you entirely pure and devoted to God; and may your spirit and soul and body be kept strong and blameless until that day when our Lord Jesus Christ comes back again" (1 Thessalonians 5:23, LB). They will need to begin the teaching early and never stop till that child is grown.

It is possible to teach our children all the justifiable, credible reasons for moral purity only to have the world give them seemingly rational, plausible reasons for doing just the opposite. The only value strong enough to combat the destructive forces of our world system is an absolute trust in God and a deep desire to obey the commands of the Bible.

Which brings us to an often neglected concept.

In this generation we have so emphasized the love of God that often we have left out the fear of God. Oh, I don't mean the fear of an angry judge sitting up there just waiting for us to do something wrong so he can punish us. I mean a healthy respect, and a fear of the consequences of disobedience—for God has promised to chasten us in love. As parents we are to nurture and to admonish—as God does His children. Usually we have no problem with the "nurture" part.

> "Unfortunately, however, within the past few generations the 'nurture' of a loving God has been so stressed that the 'admonition' of the Lord has become a matter of secondary importance. It is time that we again remember that our God of love is also a God of wrath, and that the 'admonition' of the Lord is equally important to teach.
>
> "What is the 'admonition' of the Lord? 'Admonition' speaks of instructions, of directives, of commandments. Children must learn to be disciplined; parents are instructed to discipline."[3]

As a child I knew my father loved me very much, and I loved him deeply in return. But I also had a very healthy respect for what would happen if I disobeyed or talked back to him or Mother, or struck any member of our family. There would be sudden and certain discipline. I am forever grateful for this.

There have been times in my life when nothing but the fear of God's discipline has stopped me from what I was wanting to do. This is a healthy thing.

> "Fear is a rather repugnant concept to many people, but it also is a very necessary attribute. Consider for a moment how fear enters into our everyday lives. We obey traffic laws because of a fear of consequences to ourselves and others if we don't. We treat our superiors with politeness and respect because of the fear of what might happen if we did not. We protect our children from harm because we fear they might be injured or killed. There is even an element of fear in love, if we analyze it carefully. Fear enters into a thousand different aspects of life, and fear should enter into our attitude to Almighty God. He *demands* it. 'That thou mightest fear the Lord thy God, to keep all His statutes and His commandments, which I command thee, thou, and thy son, and thy son's son, all the days of thy life; and that thy days may be prolonged'" (Deuteronomy 6:2, KJV).[4]

Of course we must not wield God's commands like a sword over the heads of our children. They must be taught first how to trust God as a loving Father and how to grow to spiritual maturity. But a part of our teaching must be a healthy respect and awe for our holy God.

Before we can teach these concepts to our children, we must know them ourselves and be gripped with the truth of Colossians 2:6-10:

> "And now just as you trusted Christ to save you, trust

Him, too, for each day's problems; live in vital union with Him.

"Let your roots grow down into Him and draw up nourishment from Him. See that you go on growing in the Lord, and become strong and vigorous in the truth you were taught. Let your lives overflow with joy and thanksgiving for all He has done.

"Don't let others spoil your faith and joy with their philosophies, their wrong and shallow answers built on men's thoughts and ideas, instead of on what Christ has said. For in Christ there is all of God in a human body; *so you have everything when you have Christ*, and you are filled with God through your union with Christ" (LB).

At this point some of you may be thinking, "How can I possibly train my children in godliness when I have failed in my own life? It is just hopeless!" No. *Never* hopeless.

Isaiah 26:12-14 says it all: "Lord, You establish peace for us; all that we have accomplished You have done for us. O Lord, our God, other lords besides You have ruled over us, but Your name alone do we honor. They are now dead, they live no more; those departed spirits do not rise. You punished them and brought them to ruin; You wiped out all memory of them" (NIV).

Isn't that something? You may have let "other lords" besides God rule over you: the lord of desire, or of impurity. These can be not only "dead," but here in Isaiah 26 God says He wipes out all *memory* of them!

When we confess our sins, God wipes them away forever. They are buried and gone. The slate is wiped clean. Oh yes, there will be scars and regrets. You will have to ask God for more of His grace not to be plagued with comparisons and guilt feelings. But God can take you, bless you, and use you in a unique way.

In the Old Testament many sins were punishable by death. The list of some of these in Leviticus 20 is awesome indeed. It was a capital offense to curse parents, commit adultery, have a homosexual relationship, or be immoral (such as a man marrying both mother and daughter). All of these were punishable by death. But remember, Christ has already died for these. In Romans 5:8 Paul tells us that "while we were yet sinners, Christ died for us." So if we have received Christ, written across these sins is the word "FORGIVEN."

That doesn't mean we should continue doing them however. God forbid! He wants our holiness of life—in a practical way—both now and forever. But for you who have scars from battered morals, ask God not only for forgiveness, but for His grace to remember them no more. Then pray for extra wisdom to train your children to follow God wholeheartedly and avoid the pitfalls into which you fell.

The prevailing thinking of our times is summed up in the statement, "What is moral is what you feel good after. What is immoral is what you feel bad after."

In a day of moral confusion, we must assert more decisively than ever that true morality is what God has revealed to be moral. Immorality is what God has revealed to be immoral.

Parents are the primary influence in the lives of their children. In a recent letter my sister said, "I was reading 1 Peter 1:4—'And to an inheritance which is imperishable, undefiled, and unfading, kept in heaven for you.' I thought of this earthly inheritance Mom and Dad left which is certainly perishable, defiled, and fading. But the other inheritance they left us—that of the knowledge of Jesus Christ as Lord and Savior and bringing us up the way they did—*that* is an inheritance we'll *never* lose and it's kept safe in heaven for us. Praise God! And raising our children to love and honor Him will be our most important inheritance left to our precious kids. We are so *blessed.*"

I heard a television speaker say recently, "It isn't what you know, it's who you know." He smiled as he repeated that well-worn phrase. The truth of it struck me that in the Christian life it isn't what you know either. It is *who* you know. The whole secret of Christlike living is wrapped up in the person of Christ. It isn't what you know to do or not to do that causes us to walk in the light, but who we know, and to what depth we know Him.

May God give us the depth to pray, the courage to teach, and the wisdom to train our children in godliness.

1. Darold A. Treffert, M.D., "Five Dangerous Ideas Our Children Have About Life," *Family Weekly*, September 19, 1976, pages 22-24.
2. Mary Susan Miller, "Teen Suicide," *Ladies Home Journal*, February 1977, pages 74-76. © 1977 LHJ Publishing, Inc., reprinted with permission.
3. C. Jackson Rayburn, M.D., "A Doctor Tells: The Blessings of Fear," *Christian Reader*, October-November 1966, pages 49-50; reprinted from the *Christian Medical Society Journal*.
4. Rayburn, "The Blessings of Fear," page 51.

PART FOUR
A Wise Woman Builds

19 The Goal of Our Lives

THREE PHONE CALLS before 10:00 A.M. that sparkling Saturday morning suddenly turned my day gloomy. Each call was from a person who was hurting, someone I cared very much about. After the third call, I returned to my room, picked up my Bible and opened it to the third chapter of Colossians. God began a process that morning of hammering home a lesson to me which He has not yet stopped. As I read, He spoke very forcefully to my heart from the first two verses: "If then you have been raised up with Christ, keep seeking the things above, where Christ is, seated at the right hand of God. Set your mind on the things above, not on the things that are on earth."

As I read in His Word, God was teaching me His ways: "Carole, you must not set your mind on anything but Me. You must keep on setting your mind and continually seeking the things which are above. Do not focus your mind on people's problems. Share their burdens, yes, but don't allow your mind to be *occupied* with these burdens. *Set your mind on Me.*" That day grew noticeably brighter.

There was more to learn—and learn, and learn.

One week after that Saturday, when a long-awaited trip overseas was cancelled, God taught me another important principle. "Carole, don't set your heart on trips on earth. Your sights aren't high enough. Set your mind on your heavenly journey. *Set your mind on Me.*" (Oh, all right Lord. That too.)

Sudden, violent storms all through the South and Midwest caused another trip to be radically altered, and God gently reminded, "Don't set your heart on a fixed schedule of events. I am in control. *Set your heart on Me.*" (Another facet? All right, Father. I think I'm getting the picture.)

And then the day came when all these pressures and problems left me teary and shaky inside. I'm not that way very often. It frightens me when I run on the fine line of tears-at-any-moment. God's persistent voice said, "Carole. One more thing. Don't set your mind on your ability or inability to be strong inside. *Set your mind on Me.*" (Was I finally getting it? It seemed as though it didn't matter whoever, whenever, whatever my focal point was. If it wasn't God, it was wrong!)

I recently read Evelyn Christenson's excellent book called *Lord, Change Me!* God spoke greatly to me through it. But I realized even there I was focusing wrongly (my fault, not hers). I was emphasizing "Lord, change *me*" and God wanted it "*Lord*, change me!"

It took several weeks for me to read past Colossians 3:1-2, because God kept stopping me right there. As I finally got to verse 3, I almost laughed out loud. There is a *reason* why things, problems, and people should not touch me. I am dead. What can touch a dead person who is perfectly hidden? This verse says I am "hidden with Christ in God." Nothing should be able to get to me.

The secret of being dead is in verse 4, which I hastened to read. My dead person is exchanged for the person of Christ, *who is my life.* I felt like shouting! An exchanged life! My dead one for His life!

This verse doesn't say that Christ is a *part* of our lives; an addition, a helper, or a friend. He *is* our life! Did I know that experientially and practically? I admitted that I needed to learn a great deal more about this particular truth. And I still do.

Part of the key goes back to verse 2: the setting of my mind, keeping my eyes, heart, and thoughts on the goal—on Him. Hebrews 12:2-3 puts it well. We are to be *"fixing our eyes* on Jesus, the author and perfecter of faith, who for the joy set before Him endured the cross, despising the shame, and has sat down at the right hand of the throne of God. For *consider* Him who has endured such hostility by sinners against Himself, so that you may not grow weary and lose heart."

We must keep our eyes on this goal.

The other night Jack and I watched a television drama called "See How She Runs." The story concerned a 40-year-old divorced teacher from Boston who decided to become a jogger, and eventually entered the 26-mile Boston Marathon. To finish the race became her goal, and in spite of being harassed, jeered at, and assaulted, she did not lose sight of it. The day of the race came and she faced her ultimate test. As she ran, huge blisters developed on her feet. She was also hit and injured by a bicycle. And several miles short of the finish line found her utterly exhausted. Yet she kept going. Then, within a few hundred yards of the finish line, late at night when most other runners had either finished or dropped out, she fell and lay flat on her face, too tired to raise her head. But her friends had put up a crude tape across the finish line and began to cheer her on. She lifted her head with great effort, saw the tape, and realized her goal was within sight. With a supreme effort she got up on her bruised and bleeding feet, and in a burst of energy dredged up from deep inside her courageous heart, she ran the last few yards.

She had kept her eyes on the goal and for the joy of finishing, she endured.

We are to do what our example, Christ, did on earth. He kept looking at the goal, not the going. He was seeing the prize, not the process; the treasure, not the trial; the joy, not the journey. And we must do the same!

Consider Jesus.

The answer to all of life is in those words. The two action verbs in Colossians 3:1-2 give us the answer to our discouragement, our fears, our frustrations. We are to *keep seeking* heavenly things—Christ Himself—and we are to *set* our minds on Him.

I am discovering that the battle is won or lost in my mind—or you may call it my will. I *choose* to lose heart, to give up, to let my mind dwell on other things. If courage is "the mental discipline to endure," then I simply decide not to endure. But I don't want to "not endure." And so goes the battle. Only God's strength and grace will win it for me.

Therein lies the key question. How, really and practically, can I keep setting my mind, and keep seeking, and keep on considering Jesus? How can I determine to endure instead of fainting? At the moment of decision, how can I ensure that I will make the right choice?

And so I searched. But not very far this time. Because Colossians 3 not only holds the "this is what to do," but also contains the "this is how you do it!" God always tells us, but sometimes I fail to look.

The answer is found in the command, "Let the word

of Christ richly dwell within you" (Colossians 3:16). I ought to know that by now! The solution lies in my day-by-day dwelling in the Word and letting the Word dwell in me. The daily battles win the war. The battle to discipline my time so I really *will* get time with God will win the war for my mind and give me the ability to continually set my mind on Him. Like the marathon runner I will probably fall many times. Perhaps this is a part of the race I cannot avoid. But to continually set my eyes back on the goal, on what Christ has for me to *be* and what He has for me eternally, this is what I want for my life.

Now between what we are to *do*—setting our minds on Him—and how we are to do it—letting the Word richly dwell in us—is what we are to *be* in relation to those around us. We are to be compassionate, kind, humble, gentle, patient, and forgiving, and we are to walk in love and be at peace (see Colossians 3:12-15). We should also have a continually thankful heart.

In other words, positionally we are dead (Colossians 3:3), hidden with Christ in God and risen with Christ. This is future. The complete truth of this in our lives will be evident when we are revealed with Christ in glory (verse 4).

Practically, we are learning to become *actually* what we already are *positionally*! (How's that for a sentence!) When we become new persons in Christ, we really are dead to immorality, idolatry, and the other things mentioned in verse 5. Most of us don't have a lot of trouble with those—at least often. But we have to continually put aside anger, wrath, malice, slander, and abusive speech (verse 8) by an act of our wills. This is the process involved in putting on our new self, and being renewed in a true knowledge of Christ (see Ephesians 4:23-24).

There are times I get very upset with the unequal way people are treated. I can feel my fighting blood beginning to boil as women are ignored, blacks are put down, or poor people are mistreated. As Christians, we should be growing in our ability to view people as God views us: that is, without distinctions (Colossians 3:11). But even this isn't going far enough. While I am to regard people without partiality or distinction, the main truth I must know is that *Christ is all and in all.* Some of us get so caught up in the fight for equality, that we forget to keep our eyes on the Master and not the battle. Christ will fight for us, or will lead us to take up the sword. The fight must not be our main concern, but our obedience to Him should be. If we were obedient and had hearts of compassion along with the other characteristics listed in Colossians 3:12-14, making no distinction between people would become automatic.

A wise woman builds into the lives of others not so much by what she does, but by who she is. In the first place, it is God who does the building in lives. In the second place, it is only as a woman's life overflows with Him that she can bear the fruit which will last (see John 15:16). What she is dictates what she does.

I am a ministry-oriented person. I like to go out "doing." But there have been several times in my life when the Lord has cut me off completely from what some call "ministry" (Bible studies, witnessing, speaking, and leading others in discipleship) in order to etch deeply in my heart that the purpose for which He created me was to know Him and to fellowship with Him. He can get along very well without my "ministry," but how wonderful it is to know that He *longs* for my fellowship! Most of all He wants me to be with Him, and to be godly, allowing the Holy Spirit full access to my life. Then He will lead me to any ministry He wants me to do, and will give me the privilege of building into the lives of those around me. I cannot help others apart from knowing Him.

Father, You know it is my desire to build up and help those around me: friends, neighbors, and others. Thank You for showing me that this building must be an overflow of Your life through me. Help me to be a clear channel for Your Spirit and to be quick to obey Your voice.

Thank You.

20 Thankfulness—in Everything

SHE WAS AN ANGELIC-LOOKING little girl who had just been very bad. Sitting on her small potty-chair in the kitchen with no one paying the slightest attention to her as we conversed, she had drawn pictures on the wall with a dark red crayon.

Her father suddenly became aware of what she had done and said quietly, "Oh, Brenda. Daddy has told you not to draw on the walls." He lifted his tiny blond daughter off her potty, took her to the basement, and saw to it that she would remember never to do it again! Then he held her until her tears ceased and he had reassured her of his love.

Sometimes our heavenly Father's lessons also hurt. But they are all taught justly and lovingly.

We can have no wisdom apart from being taught by God. He is a faithful, kind, and loving teacher *if we listen*. But in His love He will continue to be faithful—and harder—if we don't listen! I pray often that I will "learn easy." Selfishly I pray this, because I don't like hard discipline.

God never stops teaching. I find that if He doesn't show me something new about Himself or myself each week, it isn't because He has stopped teaching, but because I have stopped listening.

As I have been writing this book, God has been showing me some new things about one important attitude we must have in order to build and in order to be wise.

Have you noticed that when the Lord wants to get a point across, He seems to teach us in many ways? Specific passages of Scripture exclaim it, people mention it, and God's reproof, correction, and instruction demand it. And then in other Scripture it is sort of "tucked in" as if God were saying, "Don't forget, now!"

The attitude I'm talking about is stated forthrightly in 1 Thessalonians 5:18—"In everything give thanks; for this is God's will for you in Christ Jesus." It is also inserted among other great truths as in Philippians 4:6—"Be anxious for nothing, but in everything by prayer and supplication *with thanksgiving*, let your requests be made known to God." It must be extremely important to God for us to be thankful, because His reminders never cease!

There are some who wake up and say, "Good morning, Lord." Others are like Lucy or Linus, Charlie Schulz's lovable characters, on a "good day":[1]

God has so much more for us than "good days to be crabby!" He wants us to shout within, "THIS is the day the Lord has made. Let us rejoice and be glad in it."

God is vitally interested in our outlook and our "uplook." He wants us to have a thankful spirit for our own good. If we follow His admonition to be thankful, it is going to make the difference between a dreary existence and an exciting life. Our lives are like mirrors that are meant to shine and clearly reflect Jesus Christ. When we let those mirrors become smudged with sin, dulled with thanklessness, and dirty with despair, not only do we fail to reflect the Son, but our own souls can't grow anything beautiful either. To some, life is a trial rather than a treasure, and adversity instead of adventure. We are to look at life from above it, because that is where we are—seated with Christ "in the heavenly places" (Ephesians 2:6).

And just what *is* a positive, thankful attitude?

The story is told of a great fire in Thomas Edison's laboratories. Edison and his son rushed to the scene and watched while his life's work went up in flames. He turned to his son and exclaimed, "Son, go get your mother quick. She's never seen a fire like this!" The next morning the two were surveying the smoldering ruins and Edison said, "Just think. All our mistakes have been burned up and we have a chance to start all over again." That, to me, is a positive attitude.

Most great lessons, those deeply used by God, are learned amidst the desperate events in our lives. Since *From the Heart of a Woman*, my first book, was published, several people have remarked to me, "I didn't realize you had such a hard life." At first I reacted with amazement, because on the average I feel God has given me a truly wonderful life in every way. Then I realized that almost every chapter of the book begins with a trial! Pushed together, it looks like most of my life consisted of problems and hard circumstances. Because those were the times of deepest learning, unconsciously they became what I wrote about.

It was Paul's years in prison, his beatings, his painful times that gave him the authority to write about joy, and to encourage others.

A modern-day believer has put it this way:

"Trying circumstances are teaching ground. I've begun to realize that as we face unpleasant difficulties and situations, this is the time when God is giving us a message that we can share with others. Many times we would like to be of help to other people; we would like to have an outstanding ministry. But before we can have a ministry, we must have a message. How do we develop a message? By experiencing the reality of God in all kinds of situations. And so, even though we don't ask for them, as unpleasant and hard times come, we can learn to thank God because He will use them to our betterment.

"He will take those circumstances, which from a human standpoint are tragic, chaotic, and frustrating, and make them into that which is meaningful, building, and constructive. He will use them to conform us to the image of Christ and make us into the person we desire to be.

"As long as we resist God's will and remain bitter, discouraged, and angry, God cannot do His work in our lives. But as we submit and thank Him, we are able to learn the lessons which He wants us to know. This is a giant step toward becoming fulfilled as Christians."[2]

How tragic it is when we fail to learn God's lessons because of a negative, bitter attitude.

The men trudged homeward. They numbered an even dozen, with strong swarthy faces creased by sun and desert wind. Ten of them walked with shoulders slumped, discouragement in every step—in sharp contrast to the two others who held their heads high and spring-stepped along the dusty trail.

As they returned home a throng of people rushed to meet them and hear their report of the land which lay ahead. The ten discouraged men reported, "It's beautiful over there but we'll never make it. The people are giants and the cities are well protected. We might as well forget it!"

But the other two, Caleb and Joshua, protested: "It is a wonderful country ahead, and the Lord loves us. He will bring us safely into the land and give it to us" (Numbers 14:7-8, LB).

It has been said that "whether life grinds down a man, or polishes him, depends on what he is made of." In myself, I'm not made of very stern stuff. The "me" in me wants to grumble, complain, and murmur. I am inclined to doubt, to fear, to fail. But God in me cannot fail. He will help me face life head-on, and with joy. And I can cry with conviction, "It is a wonderful country ahead, and the Lord loves us!"

1. Copyright 1978 by United Features Syndicate, Inc., used by permission.
2. Vonette Bright, *For Such a Time as This* (Old Tappan, New Jersey: Fleming H. Revell Co., 1976), page 54.

21 The Architect and Foundation

IN MY MIND I think of them as "our mountains"—God's and mine. He made them. I enjoy them. "Our mountains" have become for me an instructive visual aid from God.

One morning as I was talking with the Lord and viewing the majesty of the mountains, I thought, *They are so strong and solid—so "forever" looking*. In that second God brought to mind that, as solid and strong as those mountains are, *I* am going to outlast them! Someday those mountains will be melted down and cast into the sea. This concept used to be beyond man's imagining. But every day in my view of the Front Range of Colorado's Rocky Mountains I see Cheyenne Mountain, beneath which lie several miles of tunnels housing the North American Air Defense Command Headquarters. In the event of an atomic war, with the capability of today's weapons, that whole mountain could be obliterated in one giant explosion following a direct hit—not a comforting thought!

But with joy I thought, *No matter. God has said I will have everlasting life because I believe in Jesus Christ.*

Whatever happens to those mountains—however long or short their life—I will outlast them, because I will live forever! My heart shouted, "Hallelujah!"

A few nights later, I stepped out onto our upstairs porch and inwardly gasped with awe. It was a perfectly still evening. The sky was velvet-soft, its blackness penetrated by a few brilliant stars. The three-quarters moon was turning the cloud it was nudging a translucent pink.

"How creative You are, Lord. You never stop creating, do You?" I asked. Then, as I gazed, the light of more and more stars began to appear, so many I could not count them. I laughed aloud (were You joining me, Lord?). I used to wonder what we would do to occupy our time in heaven. Eternity seemed endless and somewhat monotonous to me. But now I suddenly realized it would take me billions of years just to explore God's star-creations—every one quite different, just as each tiny snowflake is different.

Such a God we have!

> *"The heavens declare*
> *the glory of our God.*
> *In all the world*
> *His wonders are displayed.*
> *He traced His beauty*
> *in the earth and sky,*
> *His splendors in all things*
> *that He has made.*
> *Our God most great*
> *in majesty and power*
> *Upholding all things*
> *by the Word of His command,*
> *Has loved me*
> *with an everlasting love*

*And holds me
  in the hollow of His hand. "*[1]

One day as I was driving toward Pikes Peak, which towers above our city, the clouds were forming beautiful patterns of light and darkness on the mountains. *Forever changing*, I thought, *forever beautiful.*

"The mountains actually become more beautiful because of the shadows," I whispered aloud to the Lord as I was driving.

Quietly He answered to my heart, "So it is in your life, child of God."

Yes! The shadows, the dark times of my life, are to make my life more beautiful, more conformed to the image of God, more perfected by Him. Those shadows not only make my life more lovely to God, but also to others who are observing.

"Thank You, Lord," I murmured, "for the sunshine *and* for the shadows of my life." Such a God is mine!

It is exciting to walk with God, to let Him be the builder of our lives. I am increasingly aware that He desires to be the architect of my total life.

If I decided to build a house, I would definitely need an architect who could draw me not only an overall plan, but an extremely detailed one. What would my house look like if, after we started building, I suddenly decided I would add another room upstairs, and I later relocated a wall, exchanged a bathroom for the utility room, and put two additional hallways somewhere? When my house was finished I would no doubt have some kind of monstrosity!

To build a house I would need not only an architect, but also a master builder, because I don't even know how to drive a nail straight. If I was to be the one to actually build this house, I would have to have a very patient builder who would show me how to do *everything*, and one who would help me undo my mistakes when I put a wall up all wrong.

Now I don't know of any human architect anywhere like that. But that describes the Lord Jesus perfectly. Not only does He build our house (using our hands), but He also patiently corrects our mistakes. When we really blunder by deciding to do it our way rather than His, but are sorry for what we've done, He can even draw that horrible mistake into the plans and still have it turn out beautifully! He can make monuments out of mistakes. Given complete control, our architect—Jesus Christ—will build us a very lovely house indeed.

But a house will not stand without a foundation. And we need a very firm foundation to stand against the onslaught of the forces around us. We need Jesus Christ not only to be our architect and builder, but the foundation as well. He will not just lay a foundation, but will *become* the foundation. "For no man can lay a foundation other than the one which is laid, which is Jesus Christ" (1 Corinthians 3:11).

Life is so risky, so worthless without Him. A commuter was overheard saying to his seat companion, "I've got a clock that tells me when to get up—but some days I need one to tell me why."

We need that sure foundation to be able to know the "why" of living. We cannot build our lives on sand. We must build on the Rock. Christ is established forever in our lives as our foundation when we receive Him as our Savior and Lord.

One of my favorite stories while growing up concerned a little boy who carved a little boat with painstaking care. He sanded it and painted it a bright blue. Then he attached it to a long string and took it to a nearby creek to see if it would sail. He was thrilled that it bobbed on the water like a seagoing yacht. But suddenly a gust of wind and a stronger current caused the little boat to whirl away, and the string broke from his hand. Crestfallen, the little boy watched helplessly as his beloved boat spun from his sight around the bend where he could not follow. It was gone forever.

A week later as he was walking by a store, there in the window was his little blue boat! Joyfully he ran inside and said, "Mister, that boat in the window . . . it's mine. I made it!"

The storekeeper said, "I'm sorry, son, but I paid for that boat and if you want it, you will have to give me one dollar to buy it."

The boy lost no time running home to shake every last penny from his piggy bank. When he discovered it wasn't enough, he knocked on the doors of neighbors, asking to do some work to earn more money. He finally had the dollar, and ran back to the store and bought the boat. As he left the store with the boat lovingly cradled in his arms, he said, "Now you are twice mine. First I made you and then I bought you."

Exactly.

We are twice God's. First He made us, and the currents of sin and self whirled us away to become lost to Him. Then He bought us, redeeming us from the enemy of our souls with His own blood.

Jesus died to buy us back for God, so we might fellowship with Him.

But unlike that little blue boat, we are given a choice of whether we want to be "bought back" by God. The price has been paid, but we can refuse to be purchased. If we say "yes" to His invitation, then He becomes the foundation of our lives, the author of our salvation, the builder of eternity. If we choose not to have Him, we have nothing, but if we receive Him, we have everything. He leaves the choice with us.

1. Mary Mitchell, February 1978 calendar from Multnomah School of the Bible, Portland, Oregon.

22 The Roof over All Is Love

LYNN, AGE THREE, trudged slowly into our house, her two small ponytails sticking out at right angles to her round, troubled face. A small tear clung tenaciously to her lower lash as she hesitated before me. Then, in a sudden burst of sobs she said, "Mommy, I *spitted*!"

Confession is good for the soul they say, but this confession disturbed and confused me. Lynn had developed the unlovely habit, when confronted by something she didn't like, of spitting at the offending person. We had talked to her about this to no avail. Finally in desperation we had given her the ultimatum that if she spat again, she would have her mouth washed out with soap. I don't know why we decided this except that it worked when I was growing up!

I thought, "What do I do now?" By this time, Lynn was clinging to me and saying she was sorry over and over. From her demeanor I knew she really was. But should I say, "Okay, Honey, I forgive you" and not carry out the discipline? Would this lead to more spitting and tearful apologies? Would she then think that all she had to do was apologize and that would solve the problem without punishment? Or should I follow through with what we said would be the consequence of this disobedience? If I did, would that cause her not to be open and honest when she had disobeyed? Would it show her that truthfulness was rewarded by punishment rather than forgiveness?

No answer came to my searching mind.

So, as lovingly as I could, I said, "Honey, thank you for telling Mother. I love you and forgive you. But because I want you to remember not to ever spit again, I am going to wash your mouth out with soap." With much screaming and grimacing, the punishment was carried out.

Years later Lynn told me she had actually spat in the street after a little friend shouted at her from across the street!

I still feel awful about that one.

In pondering this later, God showed me a wonderful lesson. Have you ever wondered why, when you sin and truly repent, there is sometimes no "discipline" from the hand of God? It is gone, vanished, obliterated.

But at other times when you sin and confess it, there is still a consequence to pay, a discipline from God which comes as a result of what you did.

Why? Why on the one hand does God say, "Child, I know you are sorry. You are forgiven. It is gone," and on another occasion He says, "I know you are sorry. You are forgiven. But you must suffer the consequences of your deed"?

Well, I'm not sure of all the reasons. But I think when He doesn't discipline us, He knows not only that we are truly sorry, but that the sin would not be a problem to us again. When He does discipline us, He knows we will have continual trouble with that temptation and He is disciplining us so we will remember not to do it again.

If I had the wisdom of God when Lynn was three and could have known that she was repentant enough to never want to spit again, I could have said with confidence, "Honey, I love you and forgive you. Let's forget the whole thing." But not having that kind of wisdom, I wanted to help her not to do it again.

God's wisdom is so great! In His foreknowledge He *knows* those things for which we need discipline to help us fight future temptations.

God builds into our lives in numerous ways: through His Word, in prayer, by insights from other people, through life's experiences, and in discipline. But in every case the roof over all is love.

As we "build" into peoples' lives, love has to be our "roof" too. "Above all, keep fervent in your love for one another, because love covers a multitude of sins" (1 Peter 4:8). Love covers. It covers when friends offend me. It covers irritations, frustrations, and idiosyncrasies. And it covers both ways, doesn't it? If I really love others, I am willing and able to overlook a great many things in their lives. And if they know I love them, they are willing to overlook a great many of my faults as well. Love covers.

Let me summarize. The foundation of our house is Christ, the roof is His love, and the walls are the Word of God, prayer, obedience, fellowshipping with other Christians, witnessing. It is important to remember as we build in others' lives that these principles of walking with God are concepts that will keep the elements of the world from destroying that house. If we lay a foundation and then fail to build the walls, it is like building a foundation for a house and then finding garbage all over the foundation and spending the day cleaning up the garbage. The next day the wind has blown leaves all over the foundation so we work at sweeping off the leaves. The following week it snows and we diligently shovel off the snow. This is like dealing with problems in the lives of those comprising our "house," and failing to build the walls of the Word and prayer into their lives—concepts that will enable them to solve their own problems with the help of God alone. Otherwise their house can be destroyed by the winds of the world.

We are all in the process of building or tearing down in the lives of those around us and in our own lives. There is no possibility of maintaining the status quo. A wise woman builds. A foolish one tears down. May God grant us wisdom and teach us to number our days, to apply our hearts to His wisdom so we may present to Him a house that is a monument to His glory and useful for His service.

"We have not ceased to pray for you and to ask that you may be filled with the knowledge of His will in all spiritual wisdom and understanding, so that you may walk in a manner worthy of the Lord, to please Him in all respects, bearing fruit in every good work and increasing in the knowledge of God; strengthened with all power, according to His glorious might, for the attaining of all steadfastness and patience; joyously giving thanks to the Father, who has qualified us to share in the inheritance of the saints in light" (Colossians 1:9-12).

Father God,
How can I say 'Thank You'
for all You have done?
For opening up new truths
through Joye's illness
. . . and then giving her a
wonderful, free remission
which still exists!
For teaching me that You are wisdom:

You give wisdom;
You build wisdom;
. . . and You are more eager
for me to have it
than I am eager to receive it!
Thank You for showing me
truths about building my house.
I know it is just a beginning;
please don't stop teaching.
Thank You that You won't.
Thank You for those around me
who are "building" into me . . .
For Jack, Lynn, Tim, Joye, and
so many friends and relatives.
Thank You that they are faithful
to build, even when
their hammers hurt.
Thank You for Your love, Your patience,
Your faithfulness;
as most of all YOU build into
my life.
I love You.

Amen

Afterword: How to Apply This Book

W AIT . . . . BEFORE YOU CLOSE the pages of this book, pause to reflect with me on what we have just read. If you respond as I do after reading about such thrilling experiences, your heart is full of the hope that your life could be more like Carole's, that you too could see the "little dailies" of your life in the light of His wisdom and use them as stepping-stones to grow more like Him in every way. But I am prone to keep such longings in my thoughts for just a few weeks, and then to gradually let them fade and give way to the desires that the next book I read stimulates me to think about.

Carole did not write this book to entertain us, or to flaunt herself. The pages of this book are alive with principles that will make a permanent difference in our lives if we apply them.

As I read the opening chapters, my mind flooded with memories of the priority Carole has always given to acquiring a knowledge of the Almighty. In the late 1950s —despite the responsibilities of a young child, a household of ten to twelve people, and a growing ministry—she drove two hours every week over the busy Los Angeles freeways so we could meet together to search and discuss the Scriptures.

In the barren waters of the North Atlantic only ten percent of an iceberg is visible. The other ninety percent is under water. This is true in a sense of Carole's personal life—although she is not cold like an iceberg, but warm, loving, and caring. Her books reflect only ten percent of her character. Her pen flows freely because her life is ninety percent below the surface, characterized by her dedicated desire and disciplined pursuit to know God in His Word, and to understand His workings in her life and in the lives of those around her.

You can develop this quality of life too! The nudges of God you feel in your heart right now don't have to fade. I have always been greatly encouraged by the truth of David's words in Psalm 38:9: "Lord, all my desire is before Thee; and my sighing is not hidden from Thee." Paul wrote that "God is at work within you, helping you want to obey Him, and then helping you do what He wants" (Philippians 2:13, LB). God is waiting right now to be faithful to His promise to give us both the "want to" and the "how to" for us to please Him. God knows both our desires and our defeats, and He has the answers for our questions.

Pause right now and go to Him in prayer. Tell Him all about your longings and desires to be a wise woman. Lay the first brick in the new foundation of your house with an open commitment to make knowing Him—in a personal, in-depth way—the highest priority in your life. Write this date and the decision in the flyleaf of your Bible as a point of reference and a reminder of today's transaction.

Carole illustrates clearly that, like the iceberg, inspiration is only ten percent of accomplishment and perspiration is the other ninety percent. The goal of being a wise woman is not attained in a magical moment of chance, but in applying the knowledge of God to day-by-day living. Every woman is fully aware of the "dailyness" of her responsibilities—dishes, diapers, dirt, dressing, driving, and diet! Do you despair, as I often do, over the barrenness of busyness?

Where in the premeditated schedule of each day is there time for your spiritual growth? Our personal relationship with God can flourish only, as Carole says, through time spent with God in His Word, searching for Him as for hidden treasures, and seeking Him with our whole hearts. Take a minute now and rearrange today to reflect your commitment to being "daily His delight" (Proverbs 8:30, KJV).

Moses told us how to apply God's Word to daily living: "These commandments that I give you today are to be upon your hearts. Impress them on your children. Talk about them when you sit at home and when you walk along the road, when you lie down and when you get up" (Deuteronomy 6:6-7, NIV).

But the only commands that do you any good are the ones you know. Deciding on a specific time and place to learn them is in your hands. Before you do anything else, make room for this pursuit in your schedule. Everything must bend for it. Local Bible study groups and churches offer countless opportunities for increasing your knowledge of God and His Word. *From the Heart of a Woman*, Carole's first book, is full of practical ways for women to hear, read, study, memorize, and meditate on the Word of God for themselves.

In *Lord, Teach Me Wisdom* Carole tells us that as we increase our knowledge we gain wisdom. But few houses are built in a day. Experiencing the fruit of scriptural intake is a lifelong process. When we openly commit ourselves and make daily application of God's wisdom, we increasingly enjoy a godly lifestyle.

To my knowledge, the Mayhalls never owned a home of their own until after 24 years of marriage. But Carole was effectively building one during those years—she simply did not have a piece of real estate to put it on! She didn't wait to start her project until she had "arrived" spiritually and circumstances were perfect, or until she had a stockpile of materials and know-how. And as each brick was securely cemented into place in her own life, she shared her building secrets with others. As a result, instead of constructing only one house, she has helped put together a whole housing project. This principle was demonstrated in Chicago where Carole began meeting with one woman on a regular basis for "spiritual" building. Soon there were five ladies in the group, and later twenty. Today, Chicago's North Shore has more than 500 women who meet weekly in small Bible study groups which grew from Carole's efforts.

Pick up your trowel, perfect your skill, and watch with thanksgiving what God designs. Even if the cement is not yet dry on the first brick of your house, you can share the truth of it with someone else. By faith ask God today for an apprentice. We are not self-employed builders, but "laborers together with Him." We are responsible to the Master Builder, and "He giveth the increase." Paul's attitude in 2 Corinthians 1:24 should be our blueprint: "Not that we lord it over your faith, but are workers with you for your joy; for in your faith you are standing firm."

I am convinced that women are capable of having the kind of knowledge, wisdom, and understanding that Carole's book illustrates—if only they will choose to seek it, and follow the right path to obtain it.

"Let not the woman with college degrees boast of her intellect; neither let the woman with a charming personality boast of her congeniality; neither let the woman with a career boast of her prestige; neither let the woman with great looks boast of her beauty; neither let the woman with a Christian Dior closet boast of her wardrobe; neither let the woman who has outstanding abilities boast of her accomplishments; neither let the woman who owns a beautiful house boast of her home; neither let the woman who is involved in many clubs boast of her philanthropy; but let her who boasts boast of this alone, THAT SHE UNDERSTANDS AND KNOWS ME, that I am the Lord who exercises lovingkindness, judgment, and righteousness in the earth; for in these things I delight" (my paraphrase of Jeremiah 9:23-24).

Marion Foster
Lost Valley Ranch
Colorado